SHAMBHALA DRAGON EDITIONS

The dragon is an age-old symbol of the highest spiritual essence, embodying wisdom, strength, and the divine power of transformation. In this spirit, Shambhala Dragon Editions offers a treasury of readings in the sacred knowledge of Asia. In presenting the works of authors both ancient and modern, we seek to make these teachings accessible to lovers of wisdom everywhere.

A FLASH OF LIGHTNING IN THE DARK OF NIGHT

A Guide to the Bodhisattva's
Way of Life

Tenzin Gyatso
THE FOURTEENTH DALAI LAMA

Foreword by
Tulku Pema Wangyal

Translated from the Tibetan by
THE PADMAKARA TRANSLATION GROUP

SHAMBHALA
Boston & London
1994

Shambhala Publications, Inc.
Horticultural Hall
300 Massachusetts Avenue
Boston, Massachusetts 02115

9   8   7   6   5   4   3

Printed in the United States of America on acid-free paper ∞
Distributed in the United States by Random House, Inc.,
and in Canada by Random House of Canada Ltd

LIBRARY OF CONGRESS
CATALOGING-IN-PUBLICATION DATA
Bstan-'dzin-rgya-mtsho, Dalai Lama XIV, 1935–
A Flash of lightning in the dark of night: a guide to the
bodhisattva's way of life / Tenzin Gyatso, the Fourteenth Dalai Lama;
translated from the Tibetan by the Padmakara Translation Group.
p.   cm.—(Shambhala dragon editions)
Includes bibliographical references and index.
ISBN 0-87773-971-4
1. Śāntideva, 7th cent. Bodhicaryāvatāra.   2. Mahayana Buddhism—
Doctrines.   I. Śāntideva, 7th cent. Bodhicaryāvatāra. 1994.
II. Title.
BQ3147.B774   1994   93-36511
294.3'85—dc20   CIP

CONTENTS

Foreword   vii

Acknowledgments   ix

Translators' Note   xi

Introduction: The Way of the Bodhisattva   1

1. The Benefits of Bodhichitta   9
2. Offering and Purification   20
3. Embracing Bodhichitta   30
4. Carefulness   35
5. Attentiveness   40
6. Patience   52
7. Endeavor   75
8. Meditative Concentration   88
9. Wisdom   114
10. Dedication   124

Notes   127

Glossary   131

Bibliography   137

Index   139

FOREWORD

HIS HOLINESS THE DALAI LAMA, Tenzin Gyatso, was born in 1935 in the province of Amdo in eastern Tibet. When he was two years old he was recognized as the fourteenth in the line of Dalai Lamas, the spiritual masters who for three centuries had governed a country three times the size of France that was united and independent throughout its two-thousand-year history.

In 1950, Communist China invaded Tibet under the pretext of bringing about a "peaceful liberation." In reality what this entailed was the destruction of an entire people and its culture. Today, both are threatened with extinction.

One man, the Dalai Lama, was to become the symbol of the dramatic fight for the survival of Tibet as a nation. Since 1959, as a refugee in Dharmasala, North India, he has led and inspired the Tibetan community in exile. As a spokesman for nonviolence, he has worked untiringly for world peace. As a spiritual teacher communicating his wisdom and his experience of altruism with great simplicity, he is universally respected and venerated by millions of Buddhists who regard him as the Buddha of Compassion. For him, Buddhism is not a dogma or religion but a way of life, a source of happiness, inner peace, and wisdom. It awakens in us kindness and love, teaching us to protect every living thing on this earth. This is why he emphasizes universal responsibility, the awareness that each one of us, as a member of the human family, can be a worker for peace and a protector of the environment: "Outer disarmament comes from inner disarmament. The only true guarantee of peace lies within ourselves."

It was in this spirit that His Holiness taught for a whole week in August 1991 in Dordogne, southwestern France. Commenting on one of the greatest poetic works in Buddhist literature, Shāntideva's *Bodhicharyāvatara* (The Way of the Bodhisattva), he introduced several thousand people to the way of compassion, the path of the Bodhisattvas who, overwhelmed by the suffering of beings, take the vow to perfect themselves in order to liberate others. Despite the fact that His Holiness has given this teaching many times, so truly and fully does he live this ideal that on occasion he himself was moved to tears by the beauty of Shāntideva's text.

Just like this great Indian master of the eighth century, the Dalai Lama talks about human nature in simple and moving terms. He urges us to develop the potential we all have for love and kindness. Appealing to our everyday experience, he shows us how to become goodhearted people and give our lives direction and meaning.

TULKU PEMA WANGYAL
January 1992

ACKNOWLEDGMENTS

W E ARE MOST GRATEFUL to the Tibetan lamas who invited His Holiness the Dalai Lama to Dordogne in August 1991: Shenphen Dawa Rinpoche, Lama Jigme Rinpoche, Taklung Tsetrul Rinpoche (Tulku Pema Wangyal), and the late Nehnang Pawo Rinpoche. Because of their combined efforts, a great many people were able to meet His Holiness and attend, for the first time in France, a complete cycle of his teachings.

Members of the Padmakara Translation Group who worked on the translation of these teachings from Tibetan include Jigme Khyentse Rinpoche, Stephen Gethin, Wulstan Fletcher, Michal Abrams, Vivian Kurz, John Canti, and Kristina Permild, with invaluable additional help given by Konchog Tenzin and Christine Fondecave.

The extracts from Shāntideva's *Bodhicharyāvatara* have been printed with kind permission of the Padmakara Translation Group.

ASSOCIATION OF BUDDHIST CENTERS IN DORDOGNE

TRANSLATORS' NOTE

A LTHOUGH the Dalai Lama has become a familiar figure in
the West, with numerous publications and regular appear-
ances on television and in conference halls, this book marks
an unusual event in his visits to Europe and North America. For an
entire week, to an audience of more than two thousand people under
an enormous marquee, His Holiness gave a traditional teaching on a
great classic of Buddhist literature.

Shāntideva's *Bodhicharyāvatara* is a text covering the whole path
to enlightenment, and while it never fails to inspire, it contains sections that require detailed commentary if they are to be fully understood. A complete oral commentary can take several months, and
within the time available, it was not possible for His Holiness to
cover more than the essential points expounded by Shāntideva. In
particular, he was only able to give a brief introduction to the very
difficult ninth chapter of the text, which he intends to teach in
greater detail in November 1993. Neither was there time for him to
comment on the tenth chapter.

One or two details specific to the circumstances of the teaching
appear in this book. In the third chapter, as His Holiness explained
this part of the text, he invited those present to take the Bodhisattva
Vow, using Shāntideva's words as a basis. Chapter 10 here consists
mainly of His Holiness's concluding advice during the dedication
that marked the end of the teachings.

An attempt has been made in the translation of this book, in
both the root text and the commentary, to avoid generalized use
of masculine pronouns where Tibetan, conveniently, often uses no

pronoun at all. However, for reasons of style—particularly in the root verses where conciseness and rhythm are also important considerations—this has not always been possible. If the legendary account of Shāntideva's first delivery of this text in the eighth century is to be believed, the teaching was addressed to his fellow monks at Nālandā, and the language and examples he uses correspond to this all-male audience. In his commentary, His Holiness asks women readers to simply transpose genders when applying Shāntideva's ideas (for example in his discussion of physical desire in the eighth chapter) to their own experience.

In this book, the Dalai Lama demonstrates his profound knowledge, the fruit of the extensive training he received in the monastic centers of learning in Tibet, and his extraordinary insight into the human condition and what it means to be a responsible and good person. The simple and moving way in which he communicates the truths he exemplifies in his own life is presented within a traditional Buddhist teaching. Parts of the book contain material of a quite technical nature, requiring a basic knowledge of a number of Buddhist terms and concepts. Brief explanations of terms widely used in Buddhism have been given in the Glossary. Names and terms that appear only infrequently are commented on in endnotes.

A FLASH OF LIGHTNING
IN THE DARK OF NIGHT

The Way of the Bodhisattva

I RECEIVED the transmission of the *Bodhicharyāvatara* (The Way of the Bodhisattva) from Tenzin Gyaltsen, the Kunu Rinpoche,[1] who received it himself from a disciple of Dza Patrul Rinpoche,[2] now regarded as one of the principal spiritual heirs of this teaching. It is said that when Patrul Rinpoche explained this text auspicious signs would occur, such as the blossoming of yellow flowers, remarkable for the great number of their petals. I feel very fortunate that I am in turn able to give a commentary on this great classic of Buddhist literature.

Shāntideva composed this text in the form of an inner dialogue.[3] He turned his own weapons upon himself, doing battle with his negative emotions. Therefore, when we teach or listen to this text, it is important that we do so in order to progress spiritually, rather than making it simply a subject of academic study. With this in mind, we begin each session of teaching by paying homage to the Buddha and reciting extracts from the sūtras.

> Abandon evildoing;
> Practice virtue well;
> Subdue your mind:
> This is the Buddha's teaching.

> Like a star, an optical illusion, or a flame,
> A magical illusion, a dewdrop, or a bubble,
> Like a dream, a flash of lightning, or a cloud—
> So should one consider all compounded things.

While reciting these words, we should reflect on impermanence and the lack of reality in phenomena and conclude with a prayer of dedication:

By this merit may we attain omniscience
And overcome our enemy, our harmful deeds,
And may beings, buffeted by the waves of birth, old age,
    sickness, and death,
Be liberated from the ocean of existence.

Next we should recite the *Heart Sūtra*, the *Praise to Mañjushrī*, and the offering of the mandala.[4] Those of you who cannot recite these should simply think of the Buddha's kindness and reflect on the view of emptiness, which is the meaning of the *Prajñāpāramitā Sūtras*.

Finally, we should renew our vows, taking refuge and generating *bodhichitta* three times.

In the Jewels of the Buddha, Dharma, and Sangha,
We take refuge until we attain enlightenment.
By the merit of practicing generosity and the like,
May we attain Buddhahood for the benefit of beings.

We will now begin our study of the *Bodhicharyāvatara*.

The master of these teachings, the Buddha, began by generating the wish for enlightenment. He then accumulated positive actions through many lifetimes over a period of three great uncountable *kalpas*. Finally, in the age when the average human life span was one hundred years, he entered this world and attained enlightenment on the Vajra Throne at Bodh Gayā in India. In the twenty-five centuries since he first turned the Wheel of Dharma of the vast and profound teachings, the Buddhist path has been one of the most important of the world's spiritual traditions.[5]

I usually consider the teachings of the Buddha under two headings: activity and view. *Activity* means refraining from harming others. This is something that is universally helpful, something that all people appreciate, whether they are religious or not. *View* refers to the principle of interdependence. Happiness and suffering, and the beings who experience them, do not arise without cause nor are they caused by some eternal creator. In fact, all things arise from causes corresponding to them. This idea is upheld by all schools of Buddhism, and so I usually say that our view is that of interdependence.

The view of interdependence makes for a great openness of mind. In general, instead of realizing that what we experience arises from a complicated network of causes, we tend to attribute happiness or sadness, for example, to single, individual sources. But if this were so, as soon as we came into contact with what we consider to be good, we would be automatically happy, and conversely, in the case of bad things, invariably sad. The causes of joy and sorrow would be easy to identify and target. It would all be very simple, and there would be good reason for our anger and attachment. When, on the other hand, we consider that everything we experience results from a complex interplay of causes and conditions, we find that there is no single thing to desire or resent, and it is more difficult for the afflictions of attachment or anger to arise. In this way, the view of interdependence makes our minds more relaxed and open.

By training our minds and getting used to this view, we change our way of seeing things, and as a result we gradually change our behavior and do less harm to others. As it says in the sūtras:

> Abandon evildoing;
> Practice virtue well;
> Subdue your mind:
> This is the Buddha's teaching.

We should avoid even the smallest negative actions, and we should perform even the most insignificant positive actions without underestimating their value. The reason for this is that the happiness we all want and the suffering we all try to avoid are produced precisely by our actions, or *karma*. Everything we experience is, as it were, programmed by our actions, and these in turn depend on our attitude.

Whatever we do, say, and think in our youth is the cause of the happiness and suffering we experience in our old age. Moreover, what we do in this life will determine the happiness and suffering of the next life. And the actions of this kalpa will result in the experiences of future kalpas. This is what we mean by the law of karma, the law of cause and effect.

On this basis, an action is called negative or evil if it results in suffering, which is something we wish to avoid. It is called positive or virtuous if it results in happiness, which is something we want. We consider an action positive or negative not on its own account but according to whether it leads to joy or sorrow. This all depends on motivation, and so the text says, "Subdue your mind." A mind that is not disciplined will experience suffering, but a mind that is under control will be happy and at peace.

It is important to know all the methods for subduing the mind through the instructions of the vast and profound path. The antidote to hatred is meditation on love. To overcome attachment, we should meditate on the ugliness of what attracts us. The antidote to pride is meditation on the *skandhas*, or aggregates. To counteract ignorance we should concentrate on the movement of the breath and on interdependence. The root of the mind's turmoil is in fact ignorance, on account of which we fail to understand the true nature of things. The mind is brought under control by purifying our mistaken notion of reality. This is the teaching of the Buddha. It is through training the mind that we can transform the way in which we act, speak, and think.

It would be helpful at this point to say something about the Buddha's teaching in general. According to the Mahāyāna, after attaining enlightenment, the Buddha turned the Wheel of the Dharma, setting forth his teaching in three stages. First he taught the Four Noble Truths, on which the entire Buddhist doctrine is based. These are the truth of suffering, the truth of the origin of suffering, the truth of the cessation of suffering, and the truth of the path. With the second (or middle) turning, he gave the teachings on emptiness and the profound and detailed aspects of the path, which make up the *Prajñāpāramitā Sūtras*. With the third turning of the wheel, he presented the teachings on emptiness in a more accessible fashion. In sūtras such as the *Sūtra of Buddha Nature*, he spoke of an absolute nature that is devoid of the dualistic concept of subject and object. This is also the subject of the *Sublime Continuum*.

The origin of suffering—namely, negative emotions—may be understood with varying degrees of subtlety, and this requires an understanding of the nature of phenomena. In the second turning of the wheel, the Buddha explained in detail the truth of the cessation of suffering. He showed that an increasingly subtle analysis of phenomena leads to a greater understanding of the negative emotions and finally to an ever more refined insight into the nature of emptiness. This in turn leads to more profound understanding of the truth of the path.

In the third turning we find a detailed explanation of the path for attaining enlightenment. It emphasizes the potential that we all have for future enlightenment. This potential, called *Tathāgatagarbha*, or Buddha nature, is something we have always had, from time without beginning. When we talk about the truth of the path, we are not talking about something completely foreign to our nature, which might suddenly appear like a mushroom, as though without a seed or cause. It is because we have this foundation or capacity for ultimate omniscience that we are able to attain enlightenment.

The texts belonging to the second turning demonstrate the empty nature of phenomena, while the *Sūtra of Buddha Nature* and other teachings relating to the third turning emphasize wisdom, the clear and luminous aspect of the mind.

The Buddha taught the Four Noble Truths first, as the foundation of his whole doctrine. As he elaborated his teachings, he adapted his words to suit different needs and mental capacities. The way he taught varied considerably, and what he said was more or less profound, depending on those he was addressing. It is important, therefore, to know which teachings express the ultimate sense and which have been adapted to the particular capacities of his disciples. If, on analysis, we find that the Buddha's words, taken literally, appear illogical or lead to contradictions, we should understand that such teachings are a relative expression of the truth necessarily adapted to the comprehension of particular beings. On the other hand, if his words can be taken literally and are without any contradictions or flaws, we can accept these teachings as expressing the ultimate truth.

Faith is very important in Buddhism, but wisdom is even more so. True faith has to be based on reasoning. Simply to say, "I take refuge," or "I am devoted," blindly and without reflection, is of no value. Without rational investigation, it is impossible to distinguish whether the Buddha was speaking in an adapted, or relative, sense or whether his words are to be taken literally as expressing the ultimate meaning. This is why the sūtras mention the *four reliances:*

> Do not rely on individuals, rely on the teachings.
> Do not rely on the words, rely on the meaning.
> Do not rely on the adapted meaning, rely on the ultimate
>   meaning.
> Do not rely on intellectual knowledge, rely on wisdom.

In contrast to ordinary intellectual understanding, the true nature of the mind is clear and knowing and has never been veiled by obscurations. The practice of the Mahāyāna is entirely based on this understanding.

In Tibet, all the teachings of the Buddha, from the Four Noble Truths up to the highest yoga *tantras,* have been preserved, and are practiced in the following traditional order. The first stage is the Shrāvakayāna, or Fundamental Vehicle, the path of the Four Noble Truths. Beginning with the Vinaya,[6] which teaches the training of discipline, one progresses through the thirty-seven practices leading to enlightenment, thereby developing the two trainings of concentration and wisdom. These three trainings are the basis for the two other vehicles.

The second stage is the Mahāyāna, or Great Vehicle, and consists of the practice of the six *pāramitās*: generosity, discipline, patience, endeavor, meditative concentration, and wisdom. The third stage is the Vajrayāna, the vehicle of the secret mantras, which sets out the extraordinary means for realizing profound concentration through the union of mental calm and clear insight (*shamatha* and *vipashyanā*) and for progression through the four tantra classes: kriya, upa, yoga, and anuttara.

Buddhism has flourished for centuries in many countries, but it was in Tibet that all three paths, the Shrāvakayāna, Mahāyāna, and Vajrayāna, were preserved completely. It is, in fact, possible to go through all these stages of practice in the course of a single session. Moreover, Tibetan scholars never ignored the practice aspect, and experienced practitioners did not neglect to study. This seems to me a very good way of doing things.

In the course of time, different lineages appeared within this complete tradition, influenced by extraordinary masters who, at different times and in different places, expressed the teachings in slightly different ways.[7] We therefore have the ancient tradition of the Nyingma and the newer traditions of the Kadam, Sakya, and Kagyu. The present Gelug tradition evolved from the Kadam lineage. Despite the differences between these lineages, they all incorporate the Buddha's teachings in full, combining the practices of the Sūtrayāna and the Mahāyāna. The Bon tradition, which had existed in Tibet before the arrival of Buddhism, also came to possess a complete set of the Buddha's teachings.

The *Bodhicharyāvatara* is highly regarded by teachers of all the Tibetan schools, and perhaps as many as a hundred of them have written commentaries on it. When I received the teaching on the *Bodhicharyāvatara* from Kunu Rinpoche, he often mentioned an excellent commentary written by Minyak Kunzang Sonam,[8] a disciple of Jamyang Khyentse Wangpo.[9]

The *Bodhicharyāvatara* condenses the three turnings of the wheel of Buddha's teachings. I will read it aloud so that you receive the spiritual transmission, which is a source of blessing. I shall not explain the text word by word, but rather I shall comment on the essential points.

When receiving the teachings, it is important to have the correct attitude. It is not practicing the Dharma properly to listen with the intention of gaining material advantage or reputation. Neither should our goal be higher rebirth in the next life, as, for example, a celestial being or a powerful human being. Nor should we be wishing only for our own liberation from *saṃsāra*. These are all attitudes we should reject. Instead, let us listen to the teachings with the determined wish to attain the state of omniscience for the sake of all beings, who are infinite in number. To achieve this goal, it is necessary to practice the profound and vast path described in this text. If we can maintain this motivation, whatever positive actions we do will become the cause for supreme enlightenment. Even if such a wish does not come to us spontaneously, we can at least try to develop a positive attitude as we listen.

I

The Benefits of Bodhichitta

THE *Bodhicharyāvatara* opens with homage to the Buddhas and
Bodhisattvas, who are considered as the supreme recipients
of offerings.

1. To the Blissful Ones, who have the *dharmakāya,* and to
   all their Heirs,
   And to all who merit veneration, I bow down.
   According to tradition, I shall now in brief set forth
   An entrance to the Bodhisattva discipline.

The term *Blissful One* is synonymous with *Buddha* and is a translation of the Sanskrit *sugata.* This word is made up of two elements:
sukhā meaning "bliss," and *gata* meaning "arrived." A Sugata is therefore "one who has reached bliss," or according to the *Treatise on Logic,*
"one who has reached, or arrived, perfectly." The attainment of this
blissful state has two aspects: realization and elimination.

As the mind develops spiritual qualities and gets rid of all that
hinders them, it increasingly gains the ability to see clearly the nature
of phenomena, until it perceives the ultimate nature without any
obstruction. This perception of phenomena as they really are is the
wisdom that knows everything without the least misconception. It is
a state of wisdom that cannot be veiled, nor can it deteriorate.

The aspect of realization refers to meditation on the absence of
reality in phenomena. This leads to the perfect knowledge of the
multiplicity of phenomena and the perfect knowledge of their nature.
Then, through the power of antidotes, we eliminate all the veils that

obscure our understanding, which enables us to perceive phenomena in their naked form and attain the perfect knowledge of all phenomena without exception. These three kinds of perfect knowledge constitute the three characteristics of reaching bliss through realization.

This unmistaken view or understanding develops gradually through practice. As it becomes stronger and more evident, it acts as an antidote to the mistaken belief in ego and in the reality of phenomena, which as a result becomes weaker and weaker. Finally, when this antidote has reached its full strength, the nonconceptual wisdom that sees the *lack of self* arises.[10] This wisdom thus counteracts obscurations, and it eliminates negative emotions simply through seeing phenomena as they really are. This is what we call perfect elimination.

This is not a matter of reducing the strength of the negative emotions temporarily through meditative concentrations of differing degrees of subtlety. Once the negative emotions have been eliminated by means of nonconceptual wisdom, they are eliminated forever. They cannot recur even in situations that formerly provoked them. This is known as irreversible elimination. When the extraordinary nonconceptual wisdom is perfected through practice and all obstacles to it have been removed through the antidote, we then say that elimination is complete.

These three aspects—perfect, irreversible, and complete—are the three characteristics of realization through elimination. A Sugata, then, is one who has "arrived" through these three realizations and three eliminations.

A Sugata who has the dharmakāya starts by abandoning negative emotions, at which point he reaches the first of ten levels of the Bodhisattva path.[11] He then proceeds along the path to Buddhahood until he reaches the level of *no more learning*. At that moment, he realizes the perfectly pure absolute space, the absolute nature, and the absolute body, or dharmakāya. As obscurations to ignorance fall away, all the qualities of primordial wisdom appear, in particular the twenty-one pure qualities of the dharmakāya. What is left after all the obscurations have been eliminated is called primordial wisdom.

The realization aspect of the dharmakāya is the culmination of the truth of the path, while its elimination aspect is the culmination of the truth of cessation. Together these two truths constitute the Dharma, the second of the Three Jewels in which we take refuge. The dharmakāya is thus the ultimate aspect of the Dharma. The *sambhogakāya* and *nirmānakāya*, which manifest from the dharmakāya, constitute the Sangha of beings who have have attained the path of no more learning. And the Buddha, who is free of defects and endowed with all good qualities, is the one who possesses the truth of the path and the truth of cessation. These three—Buddha, Dharma, and Sangha—are the three absolute refuges.

The assembly of the Mahāyāna Bodhisattvas, the Shrāvakas, and the Pratyekabuddhas, who are progressing on the path, can be called the supreme community, or Sangha. It is to them, along with all other teachers worthy of veneration, that Shāntideva prostrates here.

Having paid homage to the Three Jewels, he declares his intention to compose this text, which is a compilation of the activities of the Bodhisattvas, or children of the Buddha. The Buddha is said to have three kinds of heir. His physical son was Rahūla. The heirs of his speech are the *Shrāvakas* and *Pratyekabuddhas*. And the heirs of his mind are the Bodhisattvas. These last are referred to as his principal heirs, for they aspire, for the benefit of all beings, to all the sublime qualities of Buddhahood, applying the unmistaken methods of the path of compassion and emptiness. They are the heirs of the Buddha that Shāntideva is referring to, and it is their activities, in all their different aspects, that he describes here, covering the essential points of the spiritual path.

The training of a Bodhisattva consists of the practice of the six or ten *paramitās*.[12] This can be summarized as three disciplines: avoiding harmful actions, adopting virtuous actions, and working for the benefit of beings. Shāntideva describes this path in three stages: entrance, training, and accomplishment. The entrance involves taking the Bodhisattva Vow and conceiving for the first time the aspiration for enlightenment, which is called bodhichitta. The main body of the text describes the training that follows the generation of bodhichitta, that is, the practice of the six pāramitās. The goal of this, the accomplishment of Buddhahood, is briefly described at the end of the ninth chapter.

What do we mean by *Bodhisattva*? *Bodhi* means enlightenment, the state devoid of all defects and endowed with all good qualities. *Sattva* refers to someone who has courage and confidence and who strives to attain enlightenment for the sake of all beings. Those who have this spontaneous, sincere wish to attain enlightenment for the ultimate benefit of all beings are called Bodhisattvas. Through wisdom, they direct their minds to enlightenment, and through their compassion, they have concern for beings. This wish for perfect enlightenment for the sake of others is what we call bodhichitta, and it is the starting point on the path. By becoming aware of what enlightenment is, one understands not only that there is a goal to accomplish but also that it is possible to do so. Driven by the desire to help beings, one thinks, For their sake, I must attain enlightenment! Such a thought forms the entrance to the Mahāyāna. Bodhichitta, then, is a double wish: to attain enlightenment in itself, and to do so for the sake of all beings.

One may, of course, have some vague wish to attain enlightenment, or feel it is something one ought to attain. But without having the certainty that enlightenment exists and that it is accessible, one will never accomplish it. It is therefore very important to know what enlightenment means.

In this context, the explanation of emptiness set forth in the second turning of the Wheel of Dharma is crucially important. All phenomena are by nature empty, devoid of true existence. This is clearly explained in the Prajñāpāramitā texts and the commentaries of Nāgārjuna and his followers.[13] But what is our perception of phenomena at the moment? What Nāgārjuna describes is not what we actually perceive at present. What we experience is just the opposite. Rather than perceiving phenomena as empty, we see everything as existent and real. If, through study and practice, we gain some understanding and confidence that the nature of things is emptiness, then we realize that our perceptions hitherto have not corresponded at all to the way things really are and that we have been ignorantly clinging to our mistaken way of seeing things. Moreover, this ignorance has been the root of desire and hatred; in other words, it is the very root of saṃsāra.

Ignorance, the belief that things are real, is extremely powerful. But we should remember that it is nothing more than a mistake; it is merely a misunderstanding that we cling to but which in fact has no foundation whatsoever. Its opposite, the understanding that phenomena have no reality, is based on a consistent truth that stands up to all argument. If one familiarizes oneself with this understanding, it can be developed indefinitely, since it is both true and a natural quality of the mind. As it develops and grows more powerful, it acts as the antidote to the erroneous belief that things are real, which is bound to become correspondingly weaker.

Can we get rid of this misunderstanding completely? It is said:

> The nature of mind is clear and luminous,
> But obscurations are adventitious.

Although these obscurations may have been present for a long time, they are not of the same nature as the mind. So, as the antidote—the correct perception of things—develops, these obscurations can be completely dispelled.

The nature of mind, clear and aware, is free from defects; it cannot be affected by obscurations. No phenomena, whether mental or occurring in the external world, can affect it. Nothing can alter this natural quality, which is the innate character of the mind itself. The belief in the reality of things is based on incorrect perception and is quite contrary to the mind's nature. But because of present conditions and ways of perceiving that have long grown habitual, we tend to experience things erroneously. Therefore, on the one hand, this mind that sees how things are not real is able to destroy its opposite, the conviction that phenomena are real. On the other hand, however powerful this erroneous belief in reality may be, it cannot affect the innate nature of the mind. As it is said in the *Sublime Continuum:*

> Stains are adventitious,
> Qualities are inherent.

This is very thought-provoking. Because these obscurations are in fact something separable from the mind, we can certainly get rid of them, provided we continue to practice and apply the antidotes again and again. All negative emotions can be uprooted, and since they have never penetrated the nature of the mind, even the habitual tendencies they leave behind as traces will then be eliminated.

When the mind is completely free of these negative emotions and tendencies, it understands and knows all phenomena. By exerting ourselves and using the right methods, we can actualize the potential that we have for such omniscience. It is only because there are obscuring veils between the mind and its object that we are unable to know all things. Once these veils have been removed, no new power is needed. Seeing and being aware is the nature of the mind itself. As long as the mind exists, it has the ability to know, but this ability does not reveal itself until all obscurations have been removed. This is what it means to attain enlightenment. If we think along these lines, the desire for enlightenment will grow in us.

As for the wish to work for the benefit of others, this comes from realizing that, just like ourselves, all beings, not just humans, want to be happy and not to suffer. In fact, we all have compassion: we want to free others from suffering. And to some degree, we all love and want others to be happy. These feelings may not be very strong or extensive, but everyone has them in some measure. When, for example, we see someone in agony, we spontaneously think, How terrible! and we want to relieve them of their pain. Just as we ourselves do not want to suffer but to be happy, we can have the same wish for others. Although we may have very little compassion and love at the moment, these are things that we can develop. As they grow, so also will our wish to work for others.

In order to have the desire to attain enlightenment, even if it is for our own sake, we have to know what is to be gained by being enlightened and what is lost by not being so. For this we should reflect on the imperfections of samsāra—and even those of *nirvāna* when considered as the other extreme. As it is said in the *Essence of the Middle Way:*

> Because they see its defects,
> They avoid samsāra.
> Because their hearts are loving,
> Nirvāna will not hold them.
> The wise who wish the happiness of beings
> Dwell even in samsāra.

They are not imprisoned by samsāra, as they have seen its imperfections. Because of their great compassion, they do not linger in nirvāna. As they know that there are defects in both, they aspire to an enlightenment that transcends these two extremes.

So first we have to be aware of what is wrong with samsāra, since this is the basis for the wish to attain enlightenment. To turn away and free ourselves, we must reflect on what is considered to be the suffering of samsāra; this will give rise to the desire to free others. Moreover, if we are to overcome our hopes and ambitions with respect to future existences, we must first confront our clinging to this present life. This is something we can train in, step by step.

Bodhichitta is a very good state of mind, imbued with wisdom, in which kindness is combined with the highest intelligence. It is something quite marvelous. This sort of goodness and kindness brings us peace immediately, so we are less narrow-minded and agitated. When we meet others, we do not feel claustrophobic and distant. On the contrary, we feel close to people. With a mind like this, we are never afraid, but strong and courageous. This is a very useful attitude to have.

The *Bodhicharyāvatara* is not a compilation of Shāntideva's own personal ideas, nor is it a straight repetition of the sūtras. It is rather the teachings of the sūtras in condensed form. As he says:

2. What I have to say has all been said before,
   And I am destitute of learning and of skill with words.
   I therefore have no thought that this might be of
       benefit to others.
   I wrote it only to sustain my understanding.

"What I have to say has all been said before, and I am destitute of learning and of skill with words" is said simply to ward off pride. To those who wish only to accumulate knowledge, he has nothing new to say. And as he does not think he can be of help to others, he is writing this text to further his own spiritual practice and that of those who are at the same stage as himself.

The first of the ten chapters in the *Bodhicharyāvatara* deals with the qualities of bodhichitta. As a preparation for bodhichitta, one needs to practice the seven branches so as to accumulate merit and purify oneself. This is the subject of the second chapter. The third then describes how to generate bodhichitta. The subsequent chapters explain how to put bodhichitta into practice through the six pāramitās. The first of these, generosity, is dealt with throughout the text, and there is no specific chapter devoted to it. How to practice pure discipline is explained in the two chapters on carefulness and attentiveness. These are followed by chapters devoted to the last four pāramitās: patience, endeavor, meditative concentration, and wisdom. Finally, Shāntideva concludes the text with a chapter on the dedication of merit for the benefit of beings.

Minyak Kunzang Sonam, following the tradition of Patrul Rinpoche, explains the structure of the *Bodhicharyāvatara* around Shāntideva's famous verse:

> May precious bodhichitta take its birth
> In those in whom it has not taken birth.
> And where it has been born, let it not cease
> But swell and increase ever more and more.

For those who have not yet generated bodhichitta, the first three chapters of the *Bodhicharyāvatara* explain how to do so. Then, to prevent bodhichitta from declining, there follow the instructions in the chapters on carefulness, attentiveness, and patience. After this, the chapters on endeavor, meditative concentration, and wisdom describe how bodhichitta can be continuously developed. Finally, the tenth and concluding chapter discusses how to share and dedicate this bodhichitta that has been generated, protected from decline, and increasingly developed. This is how Patrul Rinpoche explained it, and I find it very profound.

> 4. Difficult indeed to find this state of ease and
>   richness,[14]
>   Whereby the true significance of being human
>   May be reaped! If I neglect to turn it to my profit,
>   How could such a chance be mine again?

To be able to practice bodhichitta, which has so many good qualities, we need intelligence, favorable conditions, and in particular, the supreme condition of human life. A human life is difficult to find and very valuable if we have it. We should not waste our lives but should make good use of them.

> 5. As when a flash of lightning cleaves the night,
> And in its glare shows all the dark, black clouds had
>   hid,
> Likewise rarely, through the Buddhas' power,
> Virtuous thoughts rise, brief and transient, in the
>   world.

> 6. See the utter frailty of virtue!
> Except the mind of perfect bodhichitta,
> There is nothing able to withstand
> The great and overwhelming strength of evil.

Because of our past karma, it is very rare and difficult to have a positive mind, while it is all too easy to have negative thoughts, since this is what we have been used to. So we should nurture positive thoughts, such as devotion to the Buddhas and compassion for beings. It is through this that we develop bodhichitta.

There is nothing as powerful as bodhichitta for purifying our negative actions and obscurations, for attaining temporary and ultimate happiness, and for helping other beings. If we wish to free ourselves and others from the suffering of saṃsāra, then we should develop bodhichitta. As soon as we do so, its immeasurable qualities are such that, even though we may still appear to be ordinary beings subject to suffering, we will be proclaimed as heirs of the Buddhas, worthy of veneration by human and celestial beings.

Our bodhichitta may not yet be spontaneous. It is still something we have to fabricate. Nevertheless, once we have embraced and begun to develop this extraordinary attitude, whatever positive actions we do—prostration, circumambulation, recitation, or acts of generosity—while not appearing any different, will bring greatly increased results.

Bodhichitta itself has two aspects: aspiration and application. Aspiration is simply wishing to attain enlightenment for all beings, the desire to pursue the path. Application begins with taking the vow of bodhichitta and promising to put it into action. Aspiration is like simply wanting to go somewhere; application is actually going.

The good qualities of even aspiration bodhichitta are immense; how much more so are the qualities of one who has taken the vow! From the moment the vow is taken, whatever a Bodhisattva does, whether walking or sleeping, will create great merit simply through the sheer power of the intention. And if there is great merit in wanting to relieve one being of a single discomfort, need one mention the endless benefit of wishing to help innumerable beings?

It is said that to think negatively about such a Bodhisattva has extremely serious consequences. We should therefore take great care to protect ourselves from this sort of fault and consider others as our teachers. And we should never, without a very specific reason, point out other people's faults. As the omniscient Gendun Drubpa said, "Be grateful to all beings and regard all practitioners with pure vision. Subdue the enemy within."[15] Let us follow his advice.

2

Offering and Purification

According to the tradition of the Buddhadharma, training the mind is a gradual process. We purify ourselves by getting rid of our biggest defects first. And we develop good qualities by expanding on the few we already have. Āryadeva,[16] Nāgārjuna's principal disciple, said:

> First be rid of evil,
> Then be rid of self,
> Finally be rid of thoughts.
> Wise is the one who knows this.

This is the path that a wise person has to take. "First be rid of evil." To attain ultimate omniscience and be able to benefit all beings, it is necessary to have a human life, which is the supreme support for progressing toward enlightenment. To obtain a human life, which is a fortunate rebirth, it is necessary to avoid the nonvirtuous actions that will lead to birth in the lower realms of saṃsāra.

"Then be rid of self." Having forsaken negative actions, we have to abandon their causes, which are negative emotions. The only antidote to these is the wisdom that knows the nonreality of things. According to Nāgārjuna and his spiritual descendants, the root of negative emotions is the ignorance of believing that phenomena are real. This has many aspects, gross and subtle. In order to dissolve the concept of substantiality, however, we must first abandon belief in the existence of the individual as an entity, or self. But it is not enough simply to have a vague grasp of this question. It is necessary to refine our understanding and insight, and to gain that subtle wisdom whereby the notion of self is eradicated.

"Finally be rid of thoughts." To attain enlightenment, we have to remove not only negative emotions and their causes but also the habits that obscure knowledge. Once we annihilate these obscurations, we attain omniscience. The path leading to this is the wisdom that understands that things have no reality.

Through meditation we can establish firmly the view of emptiness. This extraordinary view, impregnated with compassion and combined with the accumulation of merit, completely destroys the veils that obscure knowledge. The purpose of such meditation is to act as the antidote to our own negative emotions and their traces and, indirectly, to the obscurations of all other beings. Once this goal has been achieved, all concepts, including that of emptiness, must be abandoned.

"Wise is the one who knows this." This refers to those who know the different stages of the path and its essential points and who practice them in the correct order so that they attain full realization. It is very important, therefore, to know how to practice properly and not to be satisfied with a vague or partial knowledge of the path. The *Bodhicharyāvatara* gives a complete explanation of the whole path. Please study it with the intention of bringing the infinity of sentient beings, who have been our parents, to enlightenment.[17]

If we wish to help beings, we have to be able to liberate them from suffering and dispel their ignorance. This means that we ourselves must have true realization, and this can only be achieved through endeavor and the development of clear insight and mental calm. This is how to develop relative bodhichitta and begin helping beings.

Before taking the vow of bodhichitta, we should bear in mind what it is we are aiming at and how we should proceed. We then recite the Seven Branch Prayer, with our thoughts directed to the ideal of bodhichitta.[18] The first of the Seven Branches is homage:

1. To all the Buddhas, those Thus Gone,
   To the Sacred Law, immaculate, supreme, and rare,
   And to the Buddha's heirs, an ocean of good
       qualities—
   That I might seize this precious attitude, I will make a
       perfect offering.

This is followed by the branch of offering:

2. I offer every fruit and flower,
   Every kind of healing salve,
   All the precious things the world affords,
   And all pure waters of refreshment;

3. Every mountain rich and filled with jewels,
   All sweet and lonely forest groves;
   The trees of heaven, garlanded with blossom,
   And branches heavy, laden with their fruit;

4. The perfumed fragrance of the realms of gods and
       men,
   All incense, wish-fulfilling trees, and trees of gems,
   All crops that grow without the tiller's work,
   And every sumptuous object worthy to be offered;

5. Lakes and tarns adorned with lotuses,
   And plaintive with the sweet-voiced cries of water birds
   And lovely to the eyes, and all things wild and free,
   Stretching to the boundless limits of the sky.

6. I will hold them in my mind, and to the supreme
       Buddhas
   And their heirs will make a perfect offering.
   O think of me with love, Compassionate Lords,
   Sacred objects of my gifts, accept these offerings.

Here we make an offering of everything we have along with everything else in the universe, things that are owned by someone and those that do not belong to anyone. Then we offer our own bodies. Whether or not we have a perfect body, we should offer it sincerely. This is a method of turning away from negative actions on the physical level. Next we make the offering of scented baths, celestial garments, exquisite perfumes, incense, songs of praise, and so on.

With all these offerings it is not quantity but quality that counts. Quality concerns both the materials and the intention with which they are offered. The materials offered should not be things that have been obtained dishonestly. Our intention should not be spoiled by the eight worldly preoccupations: gain or loss, pleasure or pain, praise or criticism, and fame or infamy.

When we talk about offerings that do not belong to anyone, such as all the beautiful landscapes in the world and all the different universes that have no owner, at first glance they may not seem to have anything to do with us. What is the use of mentally offering something we do not own? But in the Abhidharma it is said, "All world systems are the result of karma."[19] And according to the *Entrance to the Middle Way:*

> The infinite variety of beings and universes
> Has been created by the mind.
> All universes and beings are the result of karma.

The universe that we inhabit and our shared perception of it are the results of a common karma. Likewise, the places that we will experience in future rebirths will be the outcome of the karma that we share with the other beings living there. The actions of each of us, human or nonhuman, have contributed to the world in which we live. We all have a common responsibility for our world and are connected with everything in it. This is why we can make an offering of it.

Next comes the branch of obeisance.

24. To the Buddhas of the past, the present, and all future
    time,
    To the Doctrine and sublime Assembly,
    With bodies many as the grains of dust
    Throughout the universe, I prostrate and bow.

Prostrations are an antidote to arrogance and conceit. Before teachers begin teaching, they prostrate to the throne on which they will sit. They do this as a guard against conceit. Here we must differentiate between conceit and self-confidence. Conceit is undesirable, whereas we need to have self-confidence and the inner strength that comes from it.

The branch of confession is preceded by refuge.

26. Until the essence of enlightenment is reached,
    I will go for refuge to the Buddhas;
    Likewise, I take refuge in the Doctrine
    And the host of Bodhisattvas.

To make a proper confession, it is necessary to do so with the *four powers*. The first of these is the power of the support, which is to take refuge in the Three Jewels and to generate bodhichitta. The second power entails deep and sincere regret for all the negative actions we have done until now and the negative emotions we have indulged in. This requires reflection on the harmful effects of negative actions. The third power is the resolve never again to commit these negative actions, even if it were to cost us our lives. The fourth is the power of the antidotes, such as prostrations, recitation of mantras, and specific purificatory practices.

As well as thinking of the consequences of negative actions, we should make our confession more profound and forceful by reflecting on the inevitability of death and on the uncertainty of when it will occur. When we come to die, our future will be determined only by the positive and negative actions we have done.

> 33. Treacherous is the Lord of Death!
> Whether what we have to do is done or not,
> We cannot stay. In sickness or in health,
> We cannot trust our fleeting, flickering lives.

> 34. We must go from life forsaking everything,
> But I, devoid of sense and prudence,
> For the sake of friend and foe alike,
> Have brought about so many evils.

> 35. My enemies at length will cease to be,
> My friends and I myself
> Will cease to be,
> And all is likewise destined for destruction.

> 38. "I myself might suddenly depart,"
> Such thoughts were always far from me,
> And so, through hatred, lust, and ignorance,
> I have been the cause of many wrongs.

If we think of death in this way, we will naturally regret our past negative actions and wish to confess them immediately, feeling ill at ease until we have completely purified them. It is with such a sense of urgency in mind that Shāntideva says:

> 47. Thus from this day forth I go for refuge
> In the Buddhas, guardians of wandering beings,
> Who labor for the good of all that lives,
> Those mighty ones who scatter every fear.

The Buddha who gives us refuge has conquered the four demons: the aggregates (*skandhas*), negative emotions, death, and pride.[20] We could not, however, rely on his protection were it not for his great compassion. From the moment he generated bodhichitta until he attained enlightenment, the Buddha never ceased to work for the benefit of others, according to their individual capacities and aspirations. For this reason he is known as the Protector of Beings. So it is in this powerful, compassionate Buddha, who can dispel all fear, that from now on we take refuge. We also take refuge in his teachings and in the assembly of Bodhisattvas who have understood these teachings.

Concerning refuge in the Buddha, Dignāga[21] opens his *Compendium of Logic* thus:

> He has become authentic and knows how to help beings:
> I prostrate to the Buddha, the Sugata, the Protector.

We mean by *authentic* one who is free from suffering and fear and who knows how to free others. He helps all beings impartially and with great compassion, protecting all in need. He did not, however, appear spontaneously and without any cause, like an eternal creator. He has not always been authentic. He has become an authentic refuge as a result of definite causes and conditions, chiefly his desire to help others. When the Buddha himself was an ordinary being, wanting to be happy and to avoid suffering, he realized that these feelings were shared by all others, and he was moved by great compassion to free them from sorrow and bring about their happiness.

But to help others, it is not sufficient merely to wish to do so. Indeed, altruistic thoughts can become an obsession and increase our anxiety. When such good and positive thoughts are combined with wisdom, we know how to help beings effectively and can actually do so. The Buddha, overwhelmed by compassion, saw how beings suffer, and knowing that the cause of their suffering was the uncontrolled turbulence of their minds, he knew how to help them. He knew that their minds were uncontrolled ultimately because of ignorance, the mistaken belief in the reality of things. He knew, too, how to counteract this with the wisdom of emptiness. For a Buddha is one who knows how to help beings by showing them what they should do and what they should avoid and, above all, who reveals to them the wisdom of realizing emptiness.

For this purpose Shākyamuni Buddha taught the graded path of the Four Noble Truths with their sixteen subdivisions.[22] First he gathered around him those who had not yet started on the path and matured their minds by revealing to them impermanence and suffering, turning their thoughts away from samsāra. Then he liberated those thus matured by teaching them the nonreality of things, causing the understanding of emptiness to arise in their minds and leading them to ultimate liberation.

We call the Buddha our Teacher because he showed us what to avoid and what to take up. He himself developed the supreme wisdom that understands emptiness to the point where all dualistic perceptions disappeared, and his realization was complete. On the basis of his own experience, he was able to dispel all the sufferings of others and give them refuge. However, just as in ordinary life we would not trust someone until we had checked that what he or she said was reliable and true, in the same way, we should examine the Buddha's teachings carefully before accepting them. Broadly speaking, these teachings fall into two categories: those that show how to attain temporary happiness in higher rebirths and those that teach the path to the ultimate freedom of Buddhahood.

The *Sūtra of the Visit to Lankara* speaks of five vehicles: that of humans and celestial beings; that of Brahma; that of the Shrāvakas; that of the Pratyekabuddhas; and that of the Bodhisattvas. The first two of these are common to both Buddhist and non-Buddhist traditions. The last three are specific to the Buddhist path in their teachings on ultimate freedom and emptiness, which is what we are usually referring to when we speak of the Buddha's Doctrine.

When we examine a teaching we should analyze the principal

points. If these stand up to analysis and prove correct, then any apparent contradictions in minor details are of secondary importance. As it is said in the *Treatise on Logic*:

If the principal point is reliable,
The rest is secondary.

And the Buddha himself said:

O monks, just like examining gold in order to know its quality,
You should put my words to the test.
A wise person does not accept them merely out of respect.

Do not take the Buddha's words literally simply out of reverence. Examine them and respect them only when you have seen a good reason for doing so. Of course, faith is very important for spiritual practice, but blind devotion to the Buddha is not enough. We must have valid reasons for respecting his teachings. In the Buddhadharma, and particularly in the Mahāyāna teachings, great importance is attached to logical investigation.

The treatises on Buddhist logic talk about the fruit and its two aspects: the manifest aspect and the veiled aspect. For us ordinary beings, the fruit of Buddhahood remains obscure. If we wish to realize it without going astray, we have to take the path that unites means and wisdom, for it is based on valid principles and reflects the true nature of things.

To practice correctly, whichever path we follow, we should never go contrary to common sense. Within Buddhism there are many different teachings for beings of different dispositions and degrees of receptivity and intelligence. This is why there exist the different vehicles of the Shrāvakas, the Pratyekabuddhas, and the Bodhisattvas. For the same reason, the four philosophical schools—the Vaibhāshika, Sautrāntika, Chittamātrin, and Mādhyamika—and their numerous branches emerged to respond to different intellectual capacities.

3

Embracing Bodhichitta

I N the third chapter, which deals with the generation of bodhichitta, Shāntideva begins by rejoicing.

1. Happiness and joy I have
   In virtue, which relieves all beings
   From the sorrows of the states of grief
   And places those who languish in the realms of bliss.

2. And in that wealth of virtue I rejoice,
   Which is the cause of the enlightened state;
   Exalting in the freedom, never to be lost,
   Of living beings from the round of pain.

3. And in the Buddhahood of the Protectors I delight,
   And in the stages of the Buddhas' offspring.

4. The attitude of heart, that virtue ocean-vast,
   That brings the happiness and benefit
   Of all that lives:
   Such is my delight and all my joy.

When we rejoice in the good qualities and positive actions of others, we accumulate merit ourselves. By rejoicing in our own positive actions, we increase and strengthen their effect. On the other hand, if we show off the few good qualities that we have and are jealous of those of others, we do not even deserve to be called practicing Buddhists. So we should rejoice in all positive actions, whether of the Buddhas, Bodhisattvas, or ordinary beings.

Next comes the request for the Buddhas to turn the Wheel of Dharma and not to pass into nirvāṇa. This is followed by the dedication of merit.

> 5. I join my hands, therefore, and pray
>   The Buddhas who reside in every quarter and
>   direction,
>   To kindle now the light of Dharma
>   For those who grope bewildered in the gloom of
>   sorrow.

> 6. I join my hands likewise and pray
>   To those who have the victory and long to pass
>   Beyond the reach of sorrow: Do not leave us now in
>   ignorance,
>   Remain among us for unnumbered ages!

> 7. All these actions I have now performed,
>   And virtue I have thus amassed—
>   May all the pain of every living being
>   Be thereby scattered and destroyed!

Now begins the actual generation of bodhichitta, both aspiration and application:

> 23. Just like those, who in the past have gone to bliss,
>   Conceived the awakened attitude of mind
>   And in the precepts of the Bodhisattvas
>   Step by step abode and trained,

> 24. Likewise, for the benefit of beings,
>   I will generate this attitude of mind,

And in those self-same precepts
Step by step I will abide and train.

Aspiration bodhichitta is the vow to generate the same intention as the Buddhas and Bodhisattvas of the past. Application is the vow to accomplish, as they did, all the activities of the path to enlightenment, for the sake of all beings.

Today we shall only take the vow of aspiration. To do this, we shall read through the second and third chapters of the *Bodhicharyāvatara* up until the second line of verse 23. Try to concentrate on the meaning and afterward rejoice in what we have done.

In order to take this vow, we should imagine that in front of us are the Buddha and his eight close disciples;[23] the six ornaments,[24] and the two supreme teachers,[25] including Shāntideva; and all the realized masters of the Buddhist tradition, in particular the holders of the Sakya, Gelug, Kagyu, and Nyingma schools of Tibet—in fact, all the Buddhas and Bodhisattvas. Consider also that we are surrounded by all the beings in the universe. With this visualization, we shall now read the Seven Branch Prayer.

18. May I be a guard for those who are protectorless,
    A guide for those who journey on the road;
    For those who wish to go across the water,
    May I be a boat, a raft, a bridge.

19. May I be an isle for those who yearn for landfall,
    And a lamp for those who long for light;
    For those who need a resting place, a bed;
    For all who need a servant, may I be a slave.

20. May I be the wishing jewel, the vase of plenty,
    A word of power, and the supreme remedy.
    May I be the trees of miracles,
    And for every being, the abundant cow.

21. Like the great earth and the other elements,
    Enduring as the sky itself endures,
    For the boundless multitude of living beings,
    May I be the ground and vessel of their life.

22. Thus, for every single thing that lives,
    In number like the boundless reaches of the sky,
    May I be their sustenance and nourishment
    Until they pass beyond the bounds of suffering.

These last two lines are very powerful, are they not? The lives of a great many beings depend on the presence of the five elements, so let us think: Just like the earth, may I support beings as numerous as the sky is vast. And as long as they have not attained enlightenment, may I devote myself entirely to their happiness. Let us make a heartfelt wish to attain Buddhahood for their sake and vow never to give up this thought. If some of you are not Buddhists or feel that you are not able to keep such a vow, then you need simply think, May all beings be happy. Those of you who wish to take this vow of aspiration, please sit up straight, or kneel on your right knee, and fold your hands. Repeat after me, three times, the lines I am going to read in Tibetan. These are the first two lines of verses 23 and 24, preceded by "Teachers, Buddhas, Bodhisattvas, listen!"

I have visualized the Buddha in front of me, and you should consider that I am a sort of messenger or intermediary. Consider that we are surrounded by all the beings in the universe and generate compassion for them. Think of the Buddha and feel great devotion to him. Now, with compassion and devotion, pray, "May I attain Buddhahood!" and recite:

> Teachers, Buddhas, Bodhisattvas, listen!
> Just as you, who in the past have gone to bliss,
> Conceived the awakened attitude of mind,

Likewise, for the benefit of beings
I will generate this self-same attitude.

When we recite these lines for the third time, at the words, "I will generate this self-same attitude," think that you have generated this bodhichitta in the depth of your hearts, in the very marrow of your bones, and that you will never go back on this promise.

Traditionally we now recite the last nine verses of the chapter as a conclusion to taking the vow.

Now that we have taken this vow, we should try to be good human beings in our daily lives. We should not, for example, pretend to be very nice while we are in this tent and start fighting with each other as soon as we get out! We should from now on try to have a positive and kind mind: we are going to be happy in life. I really think that the future depends on the quality of one's mind, on a good mind. So we must try to be good people and be good examples for those around us. The initiative to be like this has to come from each one of us individually.

Thank you all for listening so carefully. I myself try to practice bodhichitta in all situations, and I try as much as possible to encourage others to do so, too. I find it is a practice that is entirely without danger and brings tremendous benefit.

4

Carefulness

THE THOUGHT of bodhichitta has now been generated in our minds. Next we come to three chapters devoted to protecting it from deterioration.

This mind of ours has the potential for accomplishing all the qualities of Buddhahood. But these qualities are temporarily obscured by our mistaken belief in the existence of an "I" and by self-centeredness and negative emotions. These are the powerful enemies of the positive attitude that we have generated. They live within our minds; they are not outside.

Were they substantial, external enemies, we might, even if they were armed with missiles, have a little time in which to run away from them. But there is no escape and nowhere to hide from these internal enemies. As circumstances arise, all sorts of negative emotions, such as desire or anger, can suddenly spring up. There are numerous antidotes for these. The most important thing, though, is to apply carefulness, attentiveness, and mindfulness. We need to be always on our guard, so that if a negative emotion or thought arises, or is about to arise, we are able to use these tools and to employ the antidote immediately, at the very moment that the mind is disturbed. When we practice in this way, with carefulness, negative emotions become less and less powerful.

Carefulness is the subject of this fourth chapter.

1. The children of the Conqueror, who thus
   Have firmly grasped this attitude of bodhichitta,

Must never turn aside from it,
Striving never to transgress its disciplines.

4. For if I bind myself with pledges
   But fail to carry out my words in deed,
   Then, each and every being thus betrayed,
   What destiny must lie in store for me?

This bodhichitta that we have generated has not been forced upon us—we have taken the bodhichitta vow voluntarily. We have taken it with all the Buddhas and Bodhisattvas as witnesses and for the sake of all beings. So to go against this vow is to show scant respect for the Buddhas and Bodhisattvas. We will have lied to them and betrayed all beings as well. This is a very serious failure.

We should therefore make every effort not to spoil our bodhichitta. We must devote all our energy to this purpose. Moreover, there is no knowing when death may overtake us. At the moment, we may be in good health, but life can end suddenly. Let us make the best use of our days, being careful all the time. It is a great mistake to be lax today, saying that we will be more strict tomorrow. We should try to discipline our minds constantly so that we can become the good people we promised to be when we took the vow. This involves watching the mind persistently.

All of us wish to be happy and do not want suffering—we do not need to be told this. But on the one hand, we do not know what we should do or avoid in order to get what makes us happy. On the other hand, because our negative emotions are so strong, we engage in negative actions even though we can see what is wrong with them. It is the emotions that are the real enemy to each of us being a good person.

28. Anger, lust—these enemies of mine—
    Are handless, footless, lacking other faculties;

They have no courage, no intelligence;
How then have they made of me their slave?

29. It is I who let them lurk within my heart,
    Allowing them to harm me at their pleasure.
    And I suffer all without resentment;
    Thus my misplaced and unworthy patience!

32. The life span of my foes, defiled emotions,
    Is never ending and has no beginning;
    Of all my other enemies,
    None have such longevity as this.

Those whom we ordinarily consider to be our enemies can only be so for one lifetime, at the most. But negative emotions have been harming us from time without beginning. They are truly the worst of enemies.

33. If my other foes I serve and cosset,
    They, in turn, will give me all their aid and favor,
    But should I serve my dark, defiled emotions,
    They will only harm and draw me back to grief.

There are always ways in which one can gradually make friends with an enemy. But the more we try to make friends with negative emotions the stronger they become and the more they are able to harm us. If we think about it, as long as they continue to inhabit our minds, staying with us like close friends, we will never be happy. As long as anger, pride, and jealousy are in our minds, we will always have external enemies. If we get rid of one enemy today, tomorrow another will appear. It is endless. While we may be able temporarily to free ourselves of enemies, with negative emotions entrenched in our minds, we shall never find lasting happiness.

43. This shall be my all-consuming passion;
    Filled with rancor, I will wage my war.
    Such emotion, though indeed defilement,
    Will destroy defilement, and I will not spurn it.

Anyone who practices the Dharma has a duty to do battle with the enemy—negative emotions. If we wish to achieve ultimate happiness, we have to use the antidote to fight against this enemy. In doing so, we may encounter difficulties from time to time. But in an ordinary war, the trials and difficulties people go through are accepted and even encourage them to fight harder against the enemy. Moreover, in the ordinary world, a warrior's wounds are considered as signs of bravery, like medals. So as practicing Buddhists fighting this real enemy, whose very nature is harm, we should expect difficulties, and treat them as signs of victory.

An ordinary enemy may escape to a safe place only to marshal his forces again and attack us once more. But once we have banished the negative emotions from our minds by using the true antidote, they have nowhere to hide and cannot return to harm us. However, we do not need anything as powerful as the nuclear arms one might use to annihilate an ordinary enemy. For negative emotions are actually impotent, based as they are on ignorance, which itself has no strength. This inner enemy is easily vanquished with the weapon of discriminating wisdom, which knows the true nature of the emotions.

47. And yet defilements are not found within the object,
    Nor yet within the faculties, nor somewhere in
        between.
    And if not elsewhere, where is their abode,
    Whence to wreak their havoc on the world?
    They are mirages, and so take heart:
    Banish fear from your mind and strive to know them.
    Why endure the needless pains of hell?

When we investigate carefully, we cannot find something, some powerful enemy, called negative emotion. In reality, there is nothing there. For example, when we experience aversion or attachment, these emotions are not located in the ugly or beautiful object that causes them, nor are they located in our own minds, nor are they to be found anywhere else. When we look more closely, we realize that it is through the coming together of causes and conditions that these emotions have such power—they do not have any power of their own. They are simply a nexus of factors that we identify and label. In fact, the emotions are entirely dependent on other things. The harm they do us is due to illusion. If we really understand this, the negative emotions cannot harm us.

What we experience within is due to external conditions coming together. If we understand that all phenomena, outer and inner, are like a dream or an illusion, then we will have revealed the weak point of our negative emotions. So to conquer them we do not need a whole arsenal of methods. We need only to recognize their nature and realize that they have no actual basis.

5

Attentiveness

1. Those who wish to keep this discipline
   Must guard their minds in perfect self-possession.
   Without this guard upon the mind,
   No discipline can ever be maintained.

HAVING TAKEN the vow of bodhichitta, we should know what are the precepts to be followed—what we have to do and what we must avoid doing. We need to be always careful in our thoughts, words, and deeds. It is here that attentiveness, or mental scrutiny, keeps us on our guard, so that when we are on the point of committing a negative action, we are aware that we are in danger of doing so and are therefore able to apply the appropriate antidote. Attentiveness is thus a watchdog, preventing us from doing anything negative. At the same time, it keeps us mindful of positive actions, so that our Bodhisattva activities increase and we are able to develop bodhichitta in all circumstances.

The spiritual training according to the monastic and lay rules of the Vinaya predominantly involves discipline of physical actions and speech, although the mind is important to the extent that it governs both of these. In the Bodhisattvayāna and Mantrayāna, on the other hand, it is the mind that is of paramount importance. The root of the Bodhisattva's discipline is to avoid any selfish attitude. We should never pursue our own interests while forgetting others or do so at the expense of others. Of course, our body and speech are involved, but we are concerned here mainly with the mind. It is within this context that a Bodhisattva, whose mind is clear, stable, and completely under control, is able to work for the benefit of others in ways that might otherwise produce harm. The main discipline, therefore, concerns the wrongdoings of the mind.

> 6. All anxiety and fear,
> Pain and suffering immeasurable,
> Each from the mind itself proceeds:
> Thus the Truthful One has said.

All suffering in this life and others is created by the unsubdued mind. Similarly, the basis of all the practices of the six pāramitās, such as generosity, moral discipline, and so on, is the mind.

> 18. This is so, and therefore I will seize
> This mind of mine and guard it well.
> What use to me so many harsh austerities?
> Let me only place a guard upon my mind.

Nothing is more important than guarding the mind. Let us constantly keep watch over the wild elephant of the mind, curbing it with mindfulness and vigilance. This is how to avoid being influenced by different external conditions. But even in retreat in a very secluded place, if the mind is not kept under control, it will wander all over the place. Even completely alone, we can have an enormous amount of negative emotions.

How are we to guard the mind? We should use attentiveness to watch our thoughts and use mindfulness to judge whether we are acting correctly. With these two we have the means to annihilate all adverse conditions. But without them, we will not see whether our thoughts are positive or negative or whether we are doing right or wrong, nor will we then be able to use antidotes as necessary.

> 23. O you who wish to place a guard upon your minds,
> I pray with palms pressed earnestly together,

At cost of life itself, preserve
Your mindfulness and mental scrutiny.

29. Therefore, from the gateway of awareness
Mindfulness shall not have leave to stray.
If it wanders, it will be recalled
By thoughts of anguish in the lower worlds.

Constantly thinking about the sufferings of the lower realms
and the results of the negative emotions will help us to develop attentiveness, mindfulness, and greater discipline. Furthermore, as Shāntideva explains:

30. In those endowed with fortune and devotion,
Mindfulness is cultivated easily
Through fear and by the counsels of their abbots
And staying ever in their teacher's company.

31. The Buddhas and the Bodhisattvas both
Possess unclouded vision, seeing everything:
All things lie before their gaze,
And likewise, I am always in their presence.

32. One who has such thoughts as these,
Will gain devotion and a sense of fear and shame.
To such a one, the memory of Buddha
Comes ever frequently to mind.

As we develop mindfulness, never forgetting what to do and
what to avoid, attentiveness gradually becomes part of us.

33. When mindfulness is stationed as a guard,
A sentinel upon the threshold of the mind,
Mental scrutiny is likewise present,
Returning when forgotten or dispersed.

In all circumstances it is necessary to evaluate the need for a particular action in relation to the precepts. According to time and circumstances, the necessity for an action may outweigh the fact that it is forbidden by the precepts, and in such circumstances we are not only permitted to transgress a vow but it is our duty to do so.[26] Indeed, there are some rules originally laid down in the Vinaya that later had to be adapted to changing circumstances.

Attentiveness should be applied to everything we do, and at all times we should be aware of our physical behavior, constantly checking whether we have been successful in doing what is proper and avoiding what is not. In this way, the mind, like a drunken elephant, maddened by the three poisons, will be tied to the pillar of positive actions with the rope of mindfulness and tamed with the hook of attentiveness.[27] If we are unable to keep the mind attuned to virtue all the time, we can let it rest in a neutral state, neither positive nor negative. But at all costs, let us avoid negative thoughts. In our meditation, when we are concentrating on specific objects, we need to be attentive and mindful all the more, for such concentration should not be distracted even by positive thoughts, let alone neutral or negative ones.

Although Bodhisattvas may be concentrating on one particular practice, they must be able to put it aside temporarily in favor of such circumstances as participating in ceremonies that benefit others, performing acts of generosity, protecting themselves if their lives are in danger, giving teachings, or accumulating merits and helping others to do so. For example, if a hunter in pursuit of a deer were to ask us if we had seen his quarry, it would be entirely admissible, in order to save the deer's life, to tell him untruthfully that we had not seen it. Here we would be giving precedence to the generosity of protecting from danger over the discipline of not telling lies. We need to evaluate such situations carefully, and we must always be on our guard to prevent negative emotions from entering our thoughts and determining our words and deeds.

It is important to be sure of our practice, clearing up all doubts and making certain that we have understood everything correctly. This confidence in the practice has to be based on clear reasoning and faith, determination and stability, and respect for the practice we are doing. Our actions should be guided by our own conscience, by concern for what others might think, and by dread of the consequences of negative actions. Keeping our senses under control, let us be peaceful and try to make others happy.

> 56. We should not be downcast by the warring wants
> Of children, to and fro. Their thoughts are bred
> From conflict and emotion.
> Let us understand and treat them lovingly.

> 57. In doing virtuous things, beyond reproach,
> To help ourselves, or for the sake of others,
> We should always bear in mind the thought
> That we are self-less, like an apparition.

Children here refers to those of immature intelligence, that is, ordinary beings with no realization. If we mix with such childish people, we risk losing our direction and will not be able to help others. So while we should avoid being influenced by them, we should not get discouraged or annoyed by them. Rather, we should feel great compassion for them, as they are in the grip of their negative emotions.

Let us try to avoid all negative actions, both those that are negative by nature and those that have been proscribed by the Buddha in connection with any vows we have taken. At the same time, let us keep foremost in our minds the intention to benefit others. For example, if allowing someone not to lose face will be the best thing for them, we should do our best to act accordingly. And all the time we should understand that we ourselves, our actions, and those who are affected by our actions are all like illusions, entirely devoid of reality.

Human life is a unique and favored opportunity and not easily gained. If we do not use it to benefit others, when will we ever get another chance? Let us value this occasion, and cultivate joy in esteeming others more than ourselves. Our determination in this should be as stable as a mountain.

Shāntideva discusses next the danger of being excessively attached to our bodies, which can prevent our doing positive actions.

61. Why not cling, O foolish mind, to something clean,
    A figure carved in wood, perhaps?
    Why do you protect and guard
    An unclean engine for the making of impurity?

62. First, with mind's imagination,
    Shed the covering skin,
    And with the blade of wisdom, strip away
    The flesh and meat from off the bones.

63. Then divide the bones,
    And scrutinize the marrow;
    Examine it and ask the question,
    Where is "thingness" to be found?

64. If, persisting in the search,
    You find no underlying object,
    Why still cherish, and with such desire,
    This fleshly form of yours?

We sometimes spend all our time looking after our bodies, to the extent that we are almost their servants. We begin the day by washing our bodies, then we feed them, and we continue to serve their needs throughout the day. But the purpose of human life is not just to sustain the body. The body is rather to be used as a vehicle for the intelligence that characterizes human existence so that we can progress spiritually. In ordinary terms, a servant who did not do what he was asked would never be paid. Factory workers lose their jobs if they do not do what they are paid for. Similarly, if our bodies, which we have fed and clothed till now, do not listen to us, this is completely wrong. The very reason we look after our bodies should be to enable us to develop a positive mind.

> 70. Regard your body as a vessel,
>   A mere boat for going here and there;
>   Make of it a wish-fulfilling gem
>   To bring about the benefit of beings.

We should use the body, which is made up of impure ingredients, to support our intention to help others. If we use it properly for our spiritual growth, combining wisdom and means, we shall be able to develop a new realization and attain the omniscient *rūpakāya* of the Tathāgatas, which is like a wish-fulfilling jewel.[28]

> 71. Thus with free, untrammeled mind,
>   Have an ever-smiling countenance.
>   Rid yourself of scowling, wrathful frowns;
>   And be a true, sincere friend to beings.

True practitioners are unaffected by external pressures and their own emotions, and they are free to secure the temporary and ultimate benefit of both themselves and others. They remain independent, fear nothing, and are never at odds with themselves. Always peaceful, they are friendly with all, and everything they say is helpful. Wherever we go, let us be humble and avoid being noisy or bossy. Let us not hurt other people's feelings or cause them to act negatively. Rather, let us be friendly and think well of others, encouraging them to accumulate positive actions.

If other people offer you advice, instead of thinking, What business is it of yours to be making suggestions? respect what they have to say and consider yourself as the disciple of all beings. If their advice is reasonable, act on it rather than arrogantly rejecting it. Show support for any positive things people say, and rejoice when you see others doing something good, encouraging them with praise. Nevertheless, if such praise is likely to appear as flattery or make them proud, praise them in private, joining in when others praise them. And if it is you whose qualities are being extolled, don't allow yourself to become proud and self-important. Simply recognize the quality others have of appreciating goodness.

The joy we can have from appreciating others' positive deeds is priceless. We stand to lose nothing from it in this life, and it is the cause of great happiness in future lives. If, on the other hand, we react negatively when other people try to correct us, or competitively when others are praised, or proudly when it is we who are praised, it will make people unhappy, and we will become lonely and friendless. And in future lives we will experience great suffering.

Whatever we say, let us speak clearly and to the point, in a voice that is calm and pleasant, unaffected by attachment or hatred. Look kindly at others, thinking, It is thanks to them that I shall attain Buddhahood.

What are the best ways to accumulate positive actions? Above all, we need a positive mind that is strong and constant. This will of itself engender positive actions. Then we must consistently apply the antidotes to desire, hatred, and ignorance. Moreover, beneficial activities are most fruitful when they are performed for learned and accomplished beings; for our parents, to whom we owe so much; for the sick, old, and weak; and for those who suffer greatly. In all these, we should not simply go along with others passively but should make an independent effort to initiate positive actions ourselves.

Our spiritual development should follow the stages of the six pāramitās, perfecting each one in turn. But we should not sacrifice a major cause of merit for a minor one. The most important thing is to keep in mind the benefit of others.

> 84. Understand this well
> And always labor for the benefit of beings.
> Those who are far-sighted and are Masters of
> Compassion
> Permit, to this end, that which is proscribed.

This verse can be interpreted in either of two ways. One meaning is that the compassionate Buddha, who sees not only the immediate but also the distant future, has seen that what is not permitted for certain beings is allowed for others. The other way of understanding this is that what is not permitted for others is allowable for the Compassionate Ones, meaning Bodhisattvas, who are endowed with wisdom and compassion.

> 85. Eating only what is needful, sharing
> With religious persons and those who are
> Defenseless or have fallen into lower states—
> Give all except the three robes of religion.

The last line of this verse concerns those who have taken monastic vows. Apart from the three monastic robes, which they should keep, any extra clothes they have should be given away for the use of others.

Now that we have dedicated our body, speech, and mind to accomplishing the sacred Dharma, we should not harm our bodies needlessly. For our bodies are the vehicles for our practice, and if we take proper care of them, we will quickly be able to fulfill the wishes of all beings.

> 87. Those should not give up their body
> Whose compassion is not pure and perfect;

Instead, in this world and the next,
They should put it to the service of the supreme goal.

In the *Compendium of All Practices* Shāntideva explains that as long
as our compassion is not completely pure and our realization of
emptiness is not perfect, it is not proper to give away our bodies and
all our wealth and merits. We need to protect our bodies, while we
purify any selfish motives we may have and increase our altruistic
attitude. If we do this, we will be able to accomplish the wishes of
all beings. Meanwhile, we should not give our lives too hastily. Instead, we should cultivate the aspiration to be able to sacrifice ourselves, until such time as doing so is truly beneficial.

The *Bodhicharyāvatara* continues with advice concerning our everyday behavior, down to how we should sleep. We should lie on
our right side with our head toward the north, as did the Buddha
when he passed into nirvāṇa, and be ready to rise promptly in the
morning.

To sum up, of all the vast activities of the Bodhisattvas the
most important is the training of the mind, which we should under-
take from the very beginning.

97. The Bodhisattva's acts
    Are boundless, as the teachings say.
    The greatest of them all is this:
    To cleanse and purify the mind.

If during the day we have committed any fault, we should ac-
knowledge it.

98. Reciting thrice by day, by night,
    The *Sūtra in Three Sections,*
    Relying on the Buddhas and the Bodhisattvas,
    I shall purify the downfalls that remain.

To be able to help beings, whose needs and dispositions are so varied, it is necessary to resort to numerous and diverse methods. Those who excel in skillful means accumulate immeasurable merits. As Shāntideva says:

100. There is no virtue
     That the Buddhas' offspring should not learn.
     To one with skill in such pursuits,
     Nothing that he does is destitute of merit.

101. Directly, then, or indirectly,
     All I do will be for others' benefit.
     And solely for their sake, I dedicate
     My actions for the gaining of enlightenment.

To make progress in our practice, we have to rely on qualified teachers, learned in the profound and vast aspects of the teachings contained in the Mahāyāna texts. Mere learning is not enough, though. Such teachers should have practiced what they have studied, incorporating it into their daily lives and combining knowledge with true spiritual realization. We should never abandon them, even if it were to cost us our lives, and we should learn how to follow them properly.

To further our understanding, Shāntideva recommends that we study other texts, such as his own *Compendium of All Practices*, which he wrote before the *Bodhicharyāvatara*. The Kadam school used to teach six principal texts, two at a time: the *Bodhisattva Levels* and *Ornament of the Mahāyāna Sūtras*, *Bodhicharyāvatara* and *Compendium of All Practices*, and *Stories of the Buddha's Series of Lives* and *Specific Counsels*. It is therefore a good idea to study the *Bodhicharyāvatara* and *Compendium of All Practices* together, as points that are treated succinctly in the one tend to be explained in detail in the other and vice versa. If we do not have time to read the *Compendium of All Practices*, Shāntideva himself advises us to study his *Compendium of All Sūtras*. However, the Tibetan translation of the latter has not survived, so we can refer instead to Nāgārjuna's text of the same name. These texts should be put fully into practice so that we can benefit others.

108. To keep a guard again and yet again
      Upon the state and actions of our minds and
          bodies—
      This alone and only this defines
      The sense of mental watchfulness.

109. All this I must express in action;
      What is to be gained by mouthing syllables?
      What invalid was ever helped
      By mere reading of the doctor's treatises?

6

Patience

THIS CHAPTER deals with patience, which together with meditative concentration, the subject of the eighth chapter, constitute the key aspects of the training in bodhichitta. The instructions contained in these two chapters are very powerful aids to practice.

1. Good works gathered in a thousand ages,
   Such as deeds of generosity,
   Or offerings to the Blissful Ones—
   A single flash of anger shatters them.

2. No evil is there similar to hatred,
   Nor austerity to be compared with patience.
   Steep yourself, therefore, in patience
   In all ways, urgently, with zeal.

As a destructive force there is nothing as strong as anger. An instant of anger can destroy all the positive actions accumulated over thousands of kalpas through the practice of generosity, making offerings to the Buddhas, keeping discipline, and so on. Indeed, there is no fault as serious as anger.

Patience, on the other hand, as a discipline that neutralizes and prevents us from succumbing to anger, is unrivaled. Through it, the suffering we endure from the heat of the negative emotions is relieved. It is therefore of the utmost importance that we resolve to practice patience, gaining inspiration through reflecting on its advantages and on the terrible effects of anger.

Here, the term *positive actions* refers to generosity, making offerings to the Buddhas and Bodhisattvas, and keeping discipline, as is explained in the *Entrance to the Middle Way*. It does not refer to the merit gained through the realization of emptiness. Anger cannot destroy this type of merit. Nor can the anger of a lower state of mind destroy the positive actions accumulated with a superior state of mind.[29] In brief, there are two types of merit that anger cannot destroy: the merit of realization of emptiness and the merit of spiritual qualities that come from meditation. Apart from these, the good effects of all other ordinary positive actions can be destroyed by anger. Nevertheless, this depends on the intensity of the anger, on the magnitude of the positive action, and on the person to whom our anger is directed. In this way, a positive action can be weakened or entirely destroyed through anger.

Positive actions are difficult to perform and therefore do not occur frequently. It is hard to have positive thoughts when one's mind is influenced by emotions and confused by adverse conditions. Negative thoughts arise by themselves, and it is difficult to make our actions truly positive when our intention and the way we carry them through are not perfectly pure. Our meager stock of hard-won positive actions is rendered powerless in an instant of anger. The damage is immeasurably more serious than if we had lost something more easily acquired.

> 3. Those tormented by the pain of anger
> Will never know tranquility of mind—
> Strangers to every joy and pleasure,
> Sleep deserts them; they will never rest.

When people get angry they lose all sense of happiness. Even if they are good-looking and normally peaceful, their faces turn livid and ugly. Anger upsets their physical well-being and disturbs their rest; it destroys their appetites and makes them age prematurely. Happiness, peace, and sleep evade them, and they no longer appreciate people who have helped them and deserve their trust and gratitude. Under the influence of anger, people of normally good character change completely and can no longer be counted on. They are ruined by their anger, and they ruin others, too. But anyone who puts all his energy into destroying anger will be happy in this life and in lives to come.

> 7. Getting what I do not want
> And that which hinders my desire—
> There my mind finds fuel for misery,
> Anger springs from it and beats me down.

When we think of someone who has wronged us or who is doing (or might do) something we or our friends dislike—depriving us of what we want—our minds, which were at peace just a moment before, suddenly become slightly agitated. This state of mind fuels negative thoughts. What an awful person! we think, and our dislike turns into hatred. It is this first stage, this unsettled feeling that kindles our hatred, that we should try to get rid of. That is why Shānti-deva says:

> 8. Therefore I will utterly destroy
> The sustenance of this my enemy,
> My foe, whose sole intention is
> To bring me sorrow.

We should try to use any means to get rid of this initial feeling of uneasiness.

> 9. Come what may, then, I will never harm
> My cheerful happiness of mind.

54

Depression never brings me what I want;
My virtue will be warped and marred by it.

10. If there is a cure when trouble comes,
What need is there for being sad?
And if no cure is to be found,
What use is there in sorrow?

We must make an effort to remain in a relaxed state of mind. Because unless we get rid of this unsettled feeling, it will feed our hatred, causing it to grow and eventually destroy us.

Anger is worse than any ordinary enemy. Of course, ordinary enemies harm us: that is why we call them enemies. But the wrong they do us is intended to help themselves or their friends, not just to make us unhappy. On the other hand, the inner enemy, anger, has no other function than to destroy our positive actions and make us suffer. That is why Shāntideva says, "My foe, whose sole intention is to bring me sorrow." From the moment it appears, it exists for the sole purpose of harming us. So we should confront it with all the means we have. Let us maintain a peaceful state of mind and avoid getting upset.

What irritates us in the first place is that our wishes are not fulfilled. But remaining upset does nothing to help fulfill those wishes. So we neither fulfill our wishes nor regain our cheerfulness! This disconcerted state, from which anger can grow, is most dangerous. We should try never to let our happy frame of mind be disturbed. Whether we are suffering at present or have suffered in the past, there is no reason to be unhappy. If we can remedy it, why be unhappy? And if we cannot, what use is there in being depressed about it? That just adds more unhappiness and does no good at all.

This initial disconcerted state, which gives rise to anger, is caused by things we do not want. For example, we do not want our friends or ourselves to suffer or be insulted, criticized, or treated with disdain. When we cannot avoid these things, we become sad. On the other hand, we feel satisfaction when it is our enemies who suffer such things, and we are not pleased when things go well for them.

> 12. The cause of happiness comes rarely,
> And many are the seeds of suffering!
> Yet if I have no pain, I'll never long for freedom.
> Therefore, O my mind, be firm!

In general we have to make a great deal of effort to obtain happiness, while suffering comes naturally. The very fact of having a body inevitably involves suffering. Sufferings are numerous and their causes abundant. A wise person can achieve happiness by transforming the causes of unhappiness into favorable conditions. We can use suffering as a means to progress. As Shāntideva says, "If I have no pain, I'll never long for freedom."

It is only natural that we dislike suffering. But if we can develop the willpower to bear difficulties, then we will grow more and more tolerant. As it is said in the text:

> 14. There is nothing that does not
> Grow easier through habit.
> Putting up with little troubles
> Will prepare me to endure much sorrow.

> 16. Heat and cold, the wind and rain,
> Sickness, prison, beatings—
> I will not fret about such things,
> For doing so will aggravate my trouble.

If we are very forbearing, then something we would normally consider very painful will not appear so bad after all. But without patient endurance, even the smallest thing becomes unbearable. A lot depends on our attitude.

17. When they see their own blood flowing,
There are some whose bravery increases,
While some grow weak and faint
Merely at the sight of others bleeding!

Similarly, if we can develop patient endurance, we will be able to bear even great difficulties when they come our way.

To be forbearing means that even when confronted with great suffering or harm we do not let it disturb our minds. Of course, it is difficult to regard sufferings as desirable and to transform them into favorable conditions. We have to be patient as we wage a determined war on negative emotions such as hatred, the worst of enemies. It is natural to expect injuries when doing battle with an ordinary enemy, so fighting the essential enemy, hatred, will not be without difficulty. But if we ignore all such ordeals and conquer negative emotions, then we can truly be called heros. On the other hand, succumbing to anger and killing an ordinary enemy is no braver than stabbing someone who is dead already. There is nothing extraordinary about that.

21. Suffering also has its value:
Through sorrow, pride is driven out
And pity felt for those who wander in saṃsāra,
Evil is drawn back from, goodness seems delightful.

Our suffering also has a positive side. For one thing, we lose our sense of self-importance. We learn to appreciate the suffering of others, and our compassion grows. And we become more careful not to accumulate the causes of suffering.

Everyone has at least some unselfish tendencies, however limited. To develop these until the wish to help others becomes limitless is what is called bodhichitta. The main obstructions to this development are the desire to harm others, resentment, and anger. To counteract these, it is therefore essential to meditate on patience. The more deeply we practice, the less chance there will be for anger to arise. Patience is the best way to avoid anger.

Now let us talk about love. In my opinion, all beings want to be loved. This is natural and spontaneous. Even animals like people who are kind to them. When someone looks at you with a loving expression, it makes you happy, does it not? Love is a quality that is esteemed throughout humanity, in all religions. All religions, including Buddhism, describe their founders above all in terms of their capacity to love. Those that talk about a creator refer to the creator's mercy. And the main quality of those who give spiritual refuge is love.

When we talk about a Pure Land filled with the presence of love, people feel like going there.[30] But were we to describe a Pure Land as a land of warfare and strife, people would no longer feel any desire to be reborn in such a place. People naturally value love, and they dislike harmful feelings and actions such as resentment, anger, fighting, stealing, coveting others' possessions, and wishing to harm others. So if love is something that all human beings prize, it is certainly something that we can develop if we make the effort.

Many people think that to be patient in bearing loss is a sign of weakness. I think this is a mistake. It is anger that is a sign of weakness, whereas patience is a sign of strength. For example, a person arguing a point based on sound reasoning remains confident and may even smile while proving his case. On the other hand, if his reasons are unsound and he is about to lose face, he gets angry, loses control, and starts talking nonsense. People rarely get angry if they are confident in what they are doing. Anger comes more easily in moments of confusion.

> 22. I'm not angry with my bile and other humors,
> Fertile source of pain and suffering!
> Why then resent my fellow creatures,
> Victims, too, of such conditions?

Suffering may result from both animate and inanimate causes. We may curse inanimate things like the weather, but it is with animate beings that we most often get angry. If we analyze these animate causes that make us unhappy, we find that they are themselves influenced by other conditions. They are not making us angry simply because they want to. In this respect, because they are influenced by other conditions, they are in fact powerless. So there is no need to get angry with them.

24. Never thinking, "Now I will be angry,"
    People are impulsively caught up in anger.
    Irritation, likewise, comes—
    Though never plans to be experienced!

25. Every injury whatever,
    The whole variety of evil deeds,
    Arise induced by circumstances.
    None are independent and autonomous.

26. Yet these causes have no thought
    Of bringing something into being.
    And that which is produced thereby
    Is mindless, with no thought of being so.

At this point in the text Shāntideva refutes the arguments of the Sāṃkhyas, one of the non-Buddhist traditions of ancient India.

27. Likewise so-called primal substance
    And the Self, whatever it may be,
    Do not come to being thinking
    As it does so, "I shall come to be."

28. Nonexistent, being not yet born,
    What could therefore want existence?

Changeless, therefore resting always in its object,
It could never cease from being so.

According to Buddhism, there is no such thing as something arising without a cause. Everything is conditioned by something else. The same applies to negative actions.

According to the Sāṃkhyas, there are twenty-five objects of knowledge, of which the principal one, the primal substance (Skt., *prakṛiti*), is considered to be absolute truth: absolute, eternal, all-pervading, and independent. All phenomena are caused by this primal substance. The Sāṃkhyas also postulated the existence of a Self, or conscious principle (*puruṣha*), that is also eternal and independent and that experiences the manifestations of the primal substance.[31]

Buddhism refutes the possibility of something independent that does not depend on a cause. Everything is interdependent. No phenomenon arises autonomously, suddenly deciding, so to speak, that it will manifest. If the primal substance were the cause of everything it gives rise to, then it would have to be produced itself. But as it is not itself created, how can it create anything?

Buddhism teaches that everything arises from causes and conditions and that therefore there is no such thing as an uncaused cause. If there were such a thing, then everything could be said to arise from nothing! Alternatively, the primal substance would have to be constantly giving rise to (causing) something. But as we can see, phenomena sometimes manifest and at other times do not. This is because the causes and conditions on which they depend sometimes come together and at other times do not.

If the cause were independent and able to create constantly, then of course its results would also have to be constant. Since the results are not constant, we can argue that their cause also is not constant: it is impermanent. If there is such a thing as an independent creator, which in consequence is alone and all-pervading, all its manifestations or results should be permanent. Belief in such a creator is simply not logical.

As regards the permanent and unchanging Self, if it were indeed immutable, all its perceptions would likewise have to be constant, and there would be no time when it was not experiencing them. Ordinary logic tells us that this is not true. Sometimes we perceive things, sometimes we do not. But perceptions would have to be permanent if the Self were an unchanging entity.

According to the *Sūtra of Interdependence*, everything arises from a cause. But such a cause cannot be a creator who at some time or other brings the universe into being. This cause is by definition impermanent, and so must itself have a cause. Finally, a result must be of the same nature as the cause that produces it. If, however, we were to believe in a permanent cause, it would be quite contradictory to believe at the same time in liberation.[32]

The Sāṃkhyas believed that the primal substance manifests saṃsāra and that the Self, which is supposed to be a permanent entity, experiences the happiness and suffering in saṃsāra. Through meditation upon the instructions of a spiritual teacher, the Self realizes that all phenomena are manifestations of the primal substance. With this realization, all the primal substance's manifestations dissolve, leaving the Self alone. This state is what the Sāṃkhyas considered to be liberation. All this is quite contradictory. If we believe that the cause of saṃsāra, the primal substance, is permanent, how can we explain liberation?

> 31. All things, then, depend on something else.
> On this depends the fact that none are independent.
> Knowing this, we will not be annoyed at objects
> That resemble magical appearances.

This is why we say that all beings are influenced by other things, meaning their own emotions, and are thus not independent. The process of cause leading to result is due to the coming together of conditions. Nothing is independent. If we understand this, then the happiness and suffering we normally perceive as real and solid will be seen as something insubstantial, like magical illusions. In light of this, we should try not to be angry with anyone.

Some people might ask, If everything is an illusion, what is the use of getting rid of illusory suffering with an antidote that is itself illusory? The answer is that illusory suffering is the result of causes and conditions that are also illusory. Even though pain is illusory, we still suffer from it, and we certainly do not want it. The same is true of happiness. It is an illusion, but it is still something we want. Thus, illusory antidotes are used to get rid of illusory sufferings, just like a magician uses one magical illusion to counteract another. This is, in fact, an important point, which is explained in greater detail in the ninth chapter of the *Bodhicharyāvatara.*

> 33. Thus, when enemies or pleasant friends
>   Are seen to act improperly,
>   Be serene and tell yourself,
>   "This comes from such and such conditions."

Let us consider that everything, whether friendly or hostile, is an illusory display, and try not to react with either attachment or anger.

> 34. If things happened solely for our pleasure,
>   How could sorrow ever come
>   To any of the host of living beings?
>   For there is no one who desires suffering.

> 38. In the grip of their defiled emotions
>   Some there are who even kill themselves:
>   Though we may be destitute of pity,
>   At least we can abstain from anger.

If we all had a choice between happiness and suffering, no one would choose suffering, and there would be no suffering in this world. But because everything is interdependent and subject to other causes, both happiness and suffering exist. People suffer without wanting to. And when the mind is not controlled, when we are influenced by hatred, we even harm ourselves. If we can harm ourselves with such hatred, we can certainly harm others.

> 39. If those who are like wanton children
> Are by nature prone to injure others,
> No use in being angry with them,
> Like resenting fire for its heat!

> 40. And if such faults are fleeting and contingent,
> If living beings are by nature wholesome,
> It is likewise senseless to be angry with them—
> As well be angry at the sky for having clouds!

We must be compassionate and never angry toward those who harm themselves. And when others harm us, we should check whether it is in their nature to do harm or simply something temporary. If it is their nature, then it is no use getting angry with them. If it is just a temporary thing, then it is not their nature that is bad, and they are simply harming us because of temporary influences. So again, it is no use getting angry with them.

If someone uses a weapon to injure us, the actual thing that hurts us is the weapon. What hurts us indirectly is the person's anger. So if we must be angry, we should be angry with the weapon or with the anger that is the reason for the weapon's being used. Take away the person's weapon and anger, and there is no one left to be angry with.

Another condition of the harming process is one's own body, which is the physical basis for suffering.

> 43. Their weapons and my body:
> Both are causes of my suffering!

They their weapons drew, while I my body
  brandished.
Who then is more worthy of my anger?

As everything is due to several causes, being angry with only
one of those causes does not make sense.

47. Those who harm me come against me
    Summoned by my evil karma.
    They will be the ones who go to hell,
    Therefore, am I not the one to injure them?

The wrongs other people do to us are the direct result of our
past actions. These actions have in fact caused our adversaries to
harm us. From this point of view, it is we who are harming our
opponents, for in the future they will suffer because of the harmful
act we ourselves have instigated.

When others harm us, it gives us the chance to practice patience
and thus to purify numerous negative actions and to accumulate
much merit. Since it is our enemies who give us this great opportunity, in reality they are helping us. But because they are committing
negative actions and we are the cause of these, we are actually harming them. So if there is anyone to get angry with, it should be ourselves. We should never be angry with our enemies, regardless of
their attitude, since they are indeed useful to us.

One might therefore wonder whether, by thus causing our enemies to accumulate negative actions, we accumulate negative actions
ourselves and whether our enemies, in so helping us to practice patience, have accumulated positive actions. This is not the case. Although we have been the cause for their negative actions, by our
practicing patience, we actually accumulate merit and will not take
rebirth in the lower realms. It is we who have been patient, and that
does not help our enemies. On the other hand, if we cannot remain

patient when we are harmed, then the harm done by our enemies will be of no help to anyone. Moreover, by losing patience and getting angry, we transgress our vow to follow the discipline of a Bodhisattva.

> 52. The mind is bodiless:
>   By no one could it be destroyed.
>   Yet it grasps the body fiercely,
>   And falls victim to the body's pain.

As the mind is not a material thing, no one can harm it. When others say unpleasant things to us, they do not hurt us physically. If we really think about this, there is nothing that is hard to bear. We might think that if we show tolerance when people say nasty things to us it will be thought that what they are saying is true and the resulting damage to our reputation will hamper our success in life. But there is nothing wrong with that. However much fame and praise we get, we can only enjoy it for this life. On the other hand, if we get angry with others, thinking they are damaging our reputation and success in this life, the negative actions we thus accumulate will follow us in our future lives.

> 62. If when others slander you, you claim
>   Your anger is because they harm themselves,
>   How is it that you do not resent
>   The slander of which others are the victim?

When people say unpleasant things about us, if it is the nasty things in themselves that make us angry, then we should get angry also when nasty things are said about others. For the case is the same as far as these unpleasant things are concerned. But when unpleasant things are said about other people, what usually happens is that we attribute the criticism to causes that do not concern us and we remain indifferent. Why do we not apply the same argument when we ourselves are the object of criticism? When someone influenced by negative emotions says nasty things about us, why do we allow ourselves to get angry? It is, after all, negative emotions, not people, that are responsible for the attack. And again, if we are not angry when other people are criticized, it follows that we should also tolerate people insulting the Buddha, breaking statues, burning down monasteries, slandering great teachers, and so on.

> 64. Even those who vilify and undermine
>   The sacred Doctrine, stupas, images of holy beings
>   Are not the proper objects of my anger:
>   The Buddhas are not harmed thereby.

> 74. For the sake of my desired aims,
>   A thousand times I have endured the fires
>   And other pains of hell,
>   Achieving nothing for myself and others.

> 75. The present pains are nothing to compare with those,
>   And yet great benefits accrue from them.
>   These afflictions, which dispel the troubles of all
>   wandering beings—
>   I should only take delight in them.

If, for example, a person condemned to death were to have his life spared in exchange for having his hands cut off, he would feel very relieved. Similarly, when we have the chance to purify a great suffering by enduring a slight injury, we should accept it. If, unable to bear insults, we get angry, we are only creating worse suffering for the future. Difficult though it may be, we should try instead to broaden our perspective and not retaliate.

We have been and are still going through endless suffering without deriving any benefit whatsoever from it. Now that we have promised to be goodhearted, we should try not to get angry when others insult us. Being patient might not be easy. It requires considerable concentration. But the result we achieve by enduring these difficulties will be sublime. That is something to be happy about!

79. When compliments are heaped upon my merits,
    I want others to rejoice in them;
    When, however, someone else is praised,
    My happiness is slow and grudging.

When people we do not like are praised, we normally become jealous. This is a mistake. When good things are said of others, we should try to join in. Then we too may get a little happiness. So why not rejoice? If we can rejoice and feel a sense of satisfaction when those we dislike are praised, the happiness we have is truly positive and approved by the Buddhas. When we practice like this, even our enemies come to appreciate us. This is one of the best ways of gaining others' respect.

80. Since I want the happiness of beings,
    I have wished to be enlightened for their sake.
    Why then should others irk me
    When they find some pleasure for themselves?

If we cannot appreciate and rejoice in the happiness someone else might have in praising other people, in the end we will be unable to tolerate even the slightest joy in anyone else. If that is the case, we might just as well give up anything that helps others and never even make gifts, refusing to accept anything that might please them. If we enjoy being praised, it is wrong for us to be irritated when someone else is praising others and deriving pleasure from doing so.

83. If even this I do not want for beings,
    How could I want Buddhahood for them?

How can anyone have bodhichitta
Who is irritated by the good that others have?

As we have taken the vow to attain omniscience for the sake of all beings, when these same beings have a little happiness on their own account, it makes sense to rejoice rather than to be irritated. We have made ourselves responsible for dispelling all suffering and accomplishing all happiness, so when others are happy our responsibility actually becomes lighter. But if we cannot bear others being happy, how can we pretend to be seeking Buddhahood?

When things are not going well for someone we dislike, what is the point in rejoicing? It does not make his present suffering any worse, and even if it did, how sad it would be that we should wish such a thing.

90. The rigmarole of praise and reputation
    Serves not to increase merit or the span of life;
    Bestowing neither health nor strength of body,
    It contributes nothing to the body's ease.

Simply being praised is of no substantial help at all: it does not increase people's good fortune, nor does it make them live any longer. If temporary pleasure is all you want, you might as well take drugs. Yet many people invest much money and even deceive their friends so as to win status. This is quite stupid. Their status and fame do not really help much in this life and do nothing for future lives. There is no point in being happy if we are famous or unhappy because people speak ill of us.

93. Children can't help crying
    When their sand castles come crumbling down.
    Our minds are so like them
    When praise and reputation start to fail.

94. Short-lived sound, devoid of intellect,
    Can never in itself intend to praise us.
    "But it's the joy that others take in me," you say.
    Are these the poor causes of your pleasure?

95. What is it to me if others should delight
    In someone else or even in myself?
    Their joy is theirs alone;
    What part of it could be for my enjoyment?

Nice words of praise are devoid of mind: they have no wish to
say good things about us. The good intentions other people have of
praising us are their good intentions, not ours! If we are happy because others have pleasant things to say about us, then we should
also be happy when they say the same about our enemies. We should
treat everyone equally.

98. Praise and compliments disturb me.
    They soften my revulsion with saṃsāra.
    I begin to covet others' qualities, and
    Every excellence is thereby spoiled.

Praise, if you think about it, is actually a distraction. For example, in the beginning one may be a simple, humble monk, content
with little. Later on, people may say flattering things like, "He's a
lama," and one begins to feel a bit more proud and to become self-
conscious about how one looks and behaves. Then the eight worldly
preoccupations become stronger, do they not? Praise is a distraction
and destroys renunciation.

Again, at first when we have little, we do not have much reason
for a sense of competition with others. But later, when the "humble
monk starts to grow some hair," he becomes conceited, and as he
becomes more influential, he vies with others for important posi-
tions. We feel jealous of anyone who has good qualities, and this in

the end destroys whatever good qualities we ourselves have. Being praised is not really a good thing, and it can be the source of negative actions.

> 99. Those who stay close by me, then,
>   To ruin my good name and cut me down to size—
>   Are they not the guardians who protect me
>   From perdition in the realms of sorrow?

As our real goal is enlightenment, we should not be angry with our enemies, who in fact dispel all the obstacles to our attaining enlightenment.

> 101. They, like Buddha's very blessing,
>   Bar my way, determined as I am
>   To plunge myself in suffering.
>   How could I be angry with them?

> 102. We should not be angry, saying,
>   "They are obstacles to virtue."
>   Patience is the peerless austerity,
>   And is this not my chosen path?

It is no use excusing ourselves, saying that our enemies are preventing us from practicing and that that is why we get angry. If we truly wish to progress, there is no practice more important than patience. We cannot pretend to be practitioners if we have no patience.

If we cannot bear the harm our enemies do to us and instead get angry, we are ourselves the obstacle to achieving an immensely positive action. Nothing can exist without a cause, and there can be no practice of patience without there being people who wrong us. How, then, can we call such people obstacles to our practice of patience, which is fundamental to the Mahāyāna path? We can hardly call a beggar an obstacle to generosity.

There are many reasons for charity; the world is full of people in need. On the other hand, those who make us angry and test our patience are relatively few, especially if we avoid harming others. So when we encounter these rare enemies we should appreciate them.

107. Like a treasure found at home,
     Enriching me without fatigue,
     Enemies are helpers in the Bodhisattva life.
     They should be a pleasure and a joy to me.

When we have been patient towards enemies, we should dedicate the fruit of this practice to them, because they are the causes of it. They have been very kind to us. We might ask, Why should they deserve this dedication when they had no intention of making us practice patience? But do objects need to have an intention before they are worthy of our respect? The Dharma itself, which points out the cessation of suffering and is the cause of happiness, has no intention of helping us, yet it is surely worthy of respect.

We might think, then, that our enemies are undeserving because they actively wish to harm us. But if everyone were as kind and well-intentioned as a doctor, how could we ever practice patience? And when a doctor, intending to cure us, hurts us by amputating a limb, cutting us open, or pricking us with needles, we do not think of him as an enemy and get angry with him. Thus, we cannot practice patience toward him. But enemies are those who intend to harm us, and it is for this reason that we are able to practice patience toward them.

111. Thanks to attitudes of bitter hatred,
     I engender patience in myself.
     They are thus the very cause of patience,
     Fit for veneration like the Doctrine.

112. Beings and the Buddhas are thus equal
    Fields of merit, said the Blessed Lord.
    Many who have sought the happiness of others,
    Have transcended all perfection.

There are two fields through which we can accumulate merit: beings and Buddhas. It is with the aid of beings, wretched though they are, that we can accumulate positive actions, develop bodhichitta, practice the six perfections, and attain the qualities of nirvāṇa. Without beings we cannot have compassion, and without compassion we cannot achieve supreme enlightenment but will rather fall into the extreme of nirvāṇa. So the attainment of supreme enlightenment and the understanding we gain on the path are dependent on beings just as much as on the Buddhas. It is a mistake to separate them, saying the Buddhas are superior and beings are inferior. As they are both equally necessary for our attainment of enlightenment, why do we not respect beings as much as we do Buddhas?

114. Their aims are not, of course, alike,
    But it is by their fruit that they must be compared.
    This, then, is the excellence of living beings' qualities.
    Beings and the Buddhas are indeed the same!

Of course, they are not equal in their qualities. But in the sense that beings have the potential to assist in our accumulating merit and gaining enlightenment, we can say that they are equal.

119. As the Buddhas are my constant friends,
    Boundless in the benefits they bring me,
    How else may I repay their goodness,
    But by making living beings happy?

122. Buddhas are made happy by the joy of beings;
    They sorrow and lament when beings suffer.

Making beings happy, I please the Buddhas also;
Offending them, the Buddhas also I offend.

If we really take refuge in the Buddhas, then we should respect their wishes. After all, in ordinary life it is normal to adapt in some way to one's friends and respect their wishes. The ability to do so is considered a good quality. It is truly sad if, on the one hand, we say that we take refuge with heartfelt devotion in the Buddha, Dharma, and Sangha, but on the other hand, in our actions, we contemptuously ignore what displeases them. We are prepared to conform to the standards of ordinary people but not to those of the Buddhas and Bodhisattvas. How miserable! If, for example, a Christian truly loves God, then he should practice love for all his fellow human beings. Otherwise, he is failing to follow his religion: his words and deeds are in contradiction.

127. Reverence for beings will rejoice the Buddhas,
     Excellently bringing welfare for myself;
     It will likewise drive away the sorrows of the world,
     And will therefore be my constant practice.

The ambassadors of a king or president, for example, have to be respected, however unimpressive they may look, because they represent a whole country. Similarly, all beings, wretched as they may be, are under the protection of the Buddhas and Bodhisattvas. So by directly harming beings, we indirectly pain the Buddhas and Bodhisattvas. This is something we should be very careful about.

If we can please beings, it goes without saying that this will contribute toward our attaining omniscience. Even in this life, we will be happy and relaxed, well thought of, and have many friends. In future lives we will be good-looking, strong, and healthy, and we will be reborn in the higher realms, with the eight qualities that are the result of positive actions. Under such favorable conditions we will eventually attain enlightenment. So helping others is fundamental on the path to Buddhahood.

This very important chapter on patience is the foundation for the eighth chapter, which shows how we can benefit others through understanding the qualities of altruism and the disadvantages of egotism.

In general it is the very notion of enemies that is the main obstacle to bodhichitta. If we can transform an enemy into someone for whom we feel respect and gratitude, then our practice will naturally progress, like water following a channel cut in the earth.

To be patient means not to get angry with those who harm us and instead to have compassion for them. That is not to say that we should let them do what they like. We Tibetans, for example, have undergone great difficulties at the hands of others. But if we get angry with them, we can only be the losers. This is why we are practicing patience. But we are not going to let injustice and oppression go unnoticed.

7

Endeavor

A FTER GENERATING bodhichitta and taking steps to prevent it from deteriorating, we must now learn to develop it continuously. This is the subject of Shāntideva's next three chapters, the first of which is devoted to endeavor.

Why is endeavor necessary? If we consider material progress, we see that research started by one person can always be continued by another. But this is not possible with spiritual progress. The realization we talk about in the Buddhadharma is something that has to be accomplished by the individual. No one else can do it for us. Of course, it would be wonderful if in the future we could attain realization through some sort of new injection or by means of a new generation of computers, without having to go through any difficulties. If we could be absolutely certain that such a time would come, we could simply lie back and wait to get enlightened. But I doubt that this will ever happen. It is better to make an effort. We have to develop endeavor.

1. Thus with patience I will practice diligence,
   For it is through zeal that I will reach enlightenment.
   If there is no wind, then nothing stirs;
   Neither is there merit where there is no diligence.

We can be patient in various ways, such as by not thinking ill of those who harm us or by accepting suffering as the path. Of these two, the latter is the more important for generating endeavor, and it is endeavor that enables us to attain enlightenment. As Shāntideva says, "It is through zeal that I will reach enlightenment." In the same way that protecting a lamp from the wind allows the flame to burn without flickering, endeavor enables the virtuous mind to grow undisturbed.

What is endeavor? It is finding joy in doing what is good. To do that, it is necessary to remove anything that counteracts it, especially laziness. Laziness has three aspects: having no wish to do good, being distracted by negative activities, and underestimating oneself by doubting one's ability. Related to these are taking undue pleasure in idleness and sleep and being indifferent to samsāra as a state of suffering.

> 4. Snared by the trapper of defiled emotion,
>   Enmeshed and taken in the toils of birth,
>   How could I not know that
>   I have fallen thus into the mouth of Death?

All of us want to be happy and to avoid suffering. But because of negative emotions, our minds are never at peace. As they arise, negative thoughts disturb our minds and create a negative atmosphere around us. Furthermore, these emotions make us liable to suffer in the future whenever we encounter difficult circumstances. While they persist, how can we tolerate them? We know that we shall die, but how can we tell when? From this moment on, we must generate endeavor.

> 7. Death will be so quick to come upon me,
>   And till that moment I must gather merits.
>   To wait till then to banish laziness—
>   What time will there be left, what shall I do?

If we wait until the moment of death to decide to make an effort, it will be too late. At that time we may be in great pain, physically and mentally, tortured by fear of the unknown, by the memory of our negative actions, and by attachment to those close to us.

8. "This I have not done. And this I'm only starting.
   And this I'm only halfway through . . ."
   Then is the sudden coming of the Lord of Death,
   And oh, the thought will come, Alas, I'm finished!

9. Your face will now be wet with tears.
   From red eyes swollen in your bitter sorrow,
   You'll gaze into the faces of your hopeless friends
   And look upon the servants of the Lord of Death.

14. Take advantage of this human boat,
    Free yourselves from sorrow's mighty stream!
    This vessel will be later hard to find;
    Now is not the time for sleep, you fool!

15. You turn your back upon the sacred Doctrine,
    The supreme joy and boundless source of happiness.
    What pleasure do you have in mere amusement
    When you stray into the causes of your misery?

Most people do not want to hear about death, let alone reflect on it. But if we have trained our minds and can face death with confidence and a fully positive attitude, then we will have nothing to fear. In the meantime, throughout our life, these qualities will help us a great deal. So while we have this precious human life, with which we can achieve so much, let us not be overwhelmed by the laziness of feeling disinclined to positive actions.

In this connection, we should consider the subject of rebirth, which Buddhism defines as the continuity of the mind from one life to the next. A future consciousness depends on a previous consciousness, of which it is the continuation. It cannot be produced by something other than consciousness. Consciousness, and not something else, must be the cause of future consciousness.

We have to understand here the distinction between gross and subtle consciousness. In general, consciousness is associated with the brain and its chemical processes. But in my opinion, it is only the gross consciousness that is determined by such factors. It is true that the gross consciousnesses related to the activities of seeing, hearing, and so forth depend on the human body and its sense organs. What we call human consciousness is the gross consciousness that uses the human body as a support. The consciousness that other forms of life, such as animals, possess is different because their brains are different.

It would be difficult, however, to prove rebirth simply on the basis of the gross consciousnesses of the different sense organs that use the brain as a support. These gross consciousnesses appear as the sense organs develop in the womb. But the consciousness that continues from life to life is a subtle consciousness—the faculty of experiencing and being aware, the natural clarity of the mind. If there were no cause for this subtle consciousness (such as the previous life's subtle consciousness), the idea of rebirth would in fact be difficult to explain.

Leaving aside memory—which allows us to remember, for example, the experiences of our youth—we all have latent and unconscious tendencies that arise under certain circumstances and influence the way our minds react. Such tendencies are the product of powerful experiences in the recent or distant past, which cause us to react unconsciously without our necessarily remembering those experiences. It is difficult to explain these tendencies and how they manifest other than by saying that they are the imprints of past experiences on the subtle consciousness.

When we talk of the big bang theory to explain the origin of the universe, as Buddhists we would have to say that the big bang itself has a cause. Everything is the product of an infinite chain of causes and effects, but we cannot in fact find an original cause to all this. There is no beginning to consciousness, to the series of our rebirths, or to the particles that make up the universe. It is simply the nature of things.

Within this context, phenomena are analyzed according to the effects they produce or according to their interdependence. Concerning analysis in terms of interdependence, we say that if the effect exists, the cause exists. This is as true for the mind as it is for particles. When we mix two chemical substances, a chemical reaction occurs and a new substance is produced. Similarly, if a very short-tempered person practices loving kindness for a long time, his character will slowly change. Of course, he may not completely get rid of his tendency to become angry, but he will be less liable to do so. This transformation of his character takes place because of the interdependence between two types of consciousness, angry and loving. Regarding analysis in terms of the effect produced, we can talk about a chemical reaction as a change of entropy. It is the same for the mind. If one contemplates the harmful effects of anger and the beneficial effects of love, one gains a new confidence in the power of love, and one's tendency to love grows stronger and stronger. This is the nature of things, and it is important to appreciate it. I don't know if this Buddhist idea of nature will satisfy everybody, but it does answer a good many questions.

To return to the subject of endeavor—if we want to get rid of the laziness of being disinclined to positive actions, we should think how short our human lives are. The Sanskrit word for laziness, *alassya*, means "not to make use of." Any positive actions we perform will benefit us now and in the future. On the other hand, letting ourselves be influenced by negative emotions will ruin us in this life and in future lives, so we should also avoid wasting our lives through the second type of laziness: being distracted by negative actions.

16. Do not be downcast, but marshal all your strength.
   Take heart and be the master of yourself.

Practice the equality of self and other;
Practice the exchange of self and other.

The third type of laziness arises from underestimating yourself and thinking you will never be able to attain enlightenment. But there is no need to be discouraged in this way. All of us have the potential for Buddhahood. The ultimate nature of the mind, though not something tangible, is present in each one of us, even when it is obscured. Because of this, even the tiniest insect can attain enlightenment if it makes the effort.

17. Oh, but how could *I* become enlightened?
    Do not be depressed by thoughts like these.
    For the Buddhas, speakers of the truth,
    Have spoken and have truly said

18. That if they bring forth strength of diligence,
    Even bees and flies and stinging gnats
    And grubs will find with ease
    Enlightenment so hard to find.

19. Able to distinguish good from ill,
    If I, by race and birth of human kind,
    Will give myself to Bodhisattva deeds,
    Why should I not gain the state of Buddhahood?

We should also not worry that we will never be able to accomplish such difficult Bodhisattva activities as giving away our bodies, possessions, and all our merits. As beginners, we may not be ready for this, so we should start by simply generating the wish to give these things and give them mentally, using the path of means and wisdom. As our practice becomes more powerful, we will arrive at a point where we know that it is appropriate to give away our bodies, and we will actually be able to do so without any physical or mental suffering.

28. Through merit they enjoy an ease of body;
    Through learning they enjoy a happiness of mind.
    Even staying in saṃsāra for the sake of beings,
    Why should those with mercy ever sorrow?

30. So now astride the horse of bodhichitta,
    Which puts to flight all mournful weariness,
    And with a mind that goes from joy to joy,
    Who could ever fall into dejection?

It is said in the *Garland of Jewels* that it is necessary to accumulate infinite merits for innumerable kalpas in order to accomplish Buddhahood. Let us not be dismayed by this, thinking, How could I ever accumulate so much merit? Instead, let us make the wish to lead infinite beings to the infinite qualities of Buddhahood by carrying out the infinite activities of the Bodhisattvas over an infinite period of time. With a single instant of such intention, having these four infinite characteristics, we can accumulate merit very easily. So let us not be influenced by the laziness of being discouraged.

31. The forces that secure the good of beings
    Are aspiration, firmness, joy, and moderation.
    Aspiration grows through contemplating misery
    And thinking of the benefit this brings.

To generate endeavor we need four supports: aspiration, firmness, joy, and moderation. Aspiration is developed by reflecting on karma, on cause and effect. As you know, a good or bad result comes from a positive action and a bad result from a negative action. So to attain the state of Buddha, who is free of all defects and endowed with all good qualities, it will be necessary to accumulate infinite merit and purify infinite obscurations over a period of many kalpas. Think how little inclined you are, in this short life, to do positive actions and to purify your obscurations. You should spur yourself to make an effort.

42. If my acts are good
    And mirror the intentions of my mind,
    No matter where I go, respect and honor
    Will be offered me, the fruit and recompense of
        merit.

43. But if, in my desire for happiness,
    All I do is wickedness instead,
    No matter where I go, the knives of misery
    Will cut me down, the wage and recompense of sin.

44. From a place within the cool heart of a fragrant,
        spreading lotus,
    Its petals opened in the Buddha's light, I shall arise
        supreme,
    With glory nourished by the sweet words of the
        Conqueror,
    And live, the Buddha's heir, within the presence of
        Victorious Ones.

The *Sūtra of the Vajra Banner* speaks about firmness, or self-confidence, in these terms: "When the sun rises, it shines over the whole world, regardless of people's blindness or mountain shadows. Likewise, when a Bodhisattva manifests for the sake of others, he brings beings to liberation, regardless of their obstacles."

Shāntideva continues with this advice:

47. First consider your resources—
    To start or not to start accordingly;

Best it is to stay and not to go,
But once you start, then better not turn back!

Before we do anything, we should always ask ourselves whether
we will be able to do it properly and complete it. If the answer is no,
we should not start. Leaving tasks uncompleted creates a habit for
the future. So once we have begun something, we should be sure not
to go back on our decision.

Self-confidence is not to be confused with pride. Pride is thinking highly of oneself without good reason. Self-confidence is knowing that one has the ability to do something properly and being
determined not to give up.

Ordinary beings are prepared to make a good deal of effort
for relatively insignificant ends. We have promised to work for the
immensely more important goal of liberating all beings, so we should
cultivate great self-confidence, thinking, Even if I am the only one to
do so, I will benefit all beings.

50. Enfeebled by their minds' afflictions,
    Worldly ones are helpless to secure their happiness.
    Compared to those who wander, I am able;
    Therefore, this shall be my task.

52. When they find a dying snake,
    Even crows behave like soaring eagles.
    If I am likewise weak and feeble,
    Even minor faults will strike and injure me.

53. How will those who leave the struggle, lily-livered,
    Ever free themselves from such debility?
    But those who confidently stand their ground and
        persevere
    Are hard to vanquish, even for the powerful.

Our resolution, however, should not involve ordinary pride, which is a negative emotion. On the contrary, we should be self-confident with regard to the negative emotions, determined not to be overcome by them.

> 55. I shall be the victor over all,
> And none shall have the victory over me!
> The lion offspring of the Conqueror
> Should constantly abide in that proud confidence.

This is the sort of pride we need—the self-confidence that does not accept the domination of the negative emotions and does everything to destroy them. The heroism of the Bodhisattva lies in this use of self-confidence to confront the negative emotions and conquer pride. People with no such self-assurance let themselves be invaded by pride and the other emotions at the slightest provocation. There is nothing heroic about that. Even if it were to cost us our lives, we should never let ourselves be influenced by these emotions.

> 61. Though tremendous danger should occur,
> A man will always move to guard his eyes.
> Likewise, though adversity befall me,
> I will not be vanquished by defiled emotion.

As regards joy, once we have generated bodhichitta, we should take up the activities of a Bodhisattva with joyful delight. The more we practice the greater should be our desire to make further progress.

> 65. If I never have enough of objects of desire,
> Sweet honey clinging to the razor's edge,
> How could I feel I ever have enough of merit,
> Which will ripen as my happiness and peace?

> 66. An elephant, tormented by the noonday sun,
> Will dive into the waters of a lake;

Likewise I must plunge into this work
That I might bring it to completion.

From one life to another we have always sought happiness, and yet, because we have always been dominated by negative emotions, we have only met with difficulties. Reborn as humans, birds, deer, insects, and so forth, we have never had lasting happiness. There has been nothing to show for all the efforts we have made to be happy and avoid suffering. Now that we have started on the Bodhisattva path, we should practice with joy and not be disheartened by the few difficulties that are bound to occur in the beginning. Our efforts will definitely bear fruit.

Moderation is to be applied when, as happens to all of us from time to time, we become physically and mentally exhausted and are unable to continue, however much we try. At such times we should not force ourselves, but we should stop and rest so that later whatever we do will be done properly and completely.

When we have rid ourselves of laziness and gained a sense of enthusiasm through our aspiration, firmness, joy, and moderation, we should practice endeavor by applying mindfulness and attentiveness. Whether during or between sessions of meditation, we must always keep our minds focused on positive actions. We might be able to meditate on bodhichitta quite well for a short while, but if we are not careful to maintain mindfulness and attentiveness all the time, we risk committing faults and transgressing our vows.

While we may concentrate on one particular aspect of the path at a time, it is important to have an overall balance between the different aspects. Meditation should progress hand in hand with study, without either one being neglected. Having cleared away doubts intellectually, we should integrate our understanding with the experience of meditation. In this way our practice will be balanced and complete.

So let us, with mindfulness and attentiveness, be careful to repel the attacks of negative emotions, putting an end to these enemies of ours so as not to slip into wrong activities.

> 69. If in the fray the soldier drops his sword,
>   In fright, he swiftly takes it up again.
>   Likewise, if the arm of mindfulness is lost,
>   In fear of hell, be quick to get it back.

Such are the dangers of becoming too relaxed and losing mindfulness.

> 70. Just as seeping venom fills the body,
>   Borne on the current of the blood,
>   Likewise, when it finds its chance,
>   Evil spreads itself throughout the mind.

On how to actually practice mindfulness and attentiveness, Shāntideva continues:

> 71. Like a fearful man, an oil jar in his hand,
>   Filled to the brim, and threatened by a swordsman
>   Saying, "Spill one drop and you shall die"—
>   This is how the disciplined should hold themselves.

> 73. At every time, then, that I make mistakes,
>   I shall reprove and vilify myself,
>   Thinking long that by whatever means
>   Such faults in future shall no more occur,

> 74. Thus at any time, in any situation,
>   Mindfulness will be my habit.
>   This will be the cause whereby I aim
>   To meet with teachers and fulfill the proper tasks.

Once we are able to practice mindfulness and attentiveness in what we do, we will never become tired or disheartened. We will always be prepared to continue.

76. The lichen hanging in the trees wafts to and fro,
    Caught in the movement of the wind.
    Likewise, all I do will be accomplished,
    Quickened by the movements of a joyful heart.

Spiritual practice is difficult in the beginning. You wonder how on earth you can ever do it. But as you get used to it, the practice gradually becomes easier. Do not be too stubborn or push yourself too hard. If you practice in accord with your individual capacity, little by little you will find more pleasure and joy in it. As you gain inner strength, your positive actions will gain in profundity and scope.

8

Meditative Concentration

1. Now that diligence has been developed,
   I will set my mind to concentrate.
   For one whose mind is loose and wandering
   Lives between the fangs of the afflictions.

TO STRENGTHEN our practice, it is necessary to develop one-pointed concentration of the mind. For this we first need to understand the disadvantages of being distracted. Lack of concentration prevents us from keeping our minds focused on the object of meditation. The mind follows any thoughts that arise, and it is then all too easy for negative emotions to grow. Any positive actions we do will not realize their full effect. Distraction is therefore a major defect, and it is very important to counteract it by developing mental calm (*shamatha*).

The practice of mental calm is not unique to Buddhism. Non-Buddhist traditions include methods for developing mental calm through which it is possible to attain the state of concentration of the formless celestial beings (*devas*) in the realm of *nothing at all*.[33] In this state negative emotions are allayed but not entirely eliminated—they remain latent. Mental calm on its own, therefore, is not uniquely special. But this one-pointed concentration is very important in developing fully the power of positive actions, and it is crucial for our practice of clear insight (*vipashyana*). The Mādhyamika view, which is common to both Sūtrayāna and Mantrayāna, is established through analytical reasoning until we obtain certainty in it.[34] This is something very subtle, and unless our power of concentration is stable, there is a danger of losing this view of emptiness. The more stable our concentration is, the clearer will be our understanding of emptiness.

What do we mean by meditation? First, there is meditation through analysis, whereby we repeatedly examine an object until we gain a degree of certainty concerning its nature. When we cannot proceed any further with analysis, we let ourselves repose in the state of clarity and confidence that we have achieved. This is placement meditation. It is the latter type of meditation that is used in practices such as visualizing deities and training in mental calm, where one is developing the power of concentration.

One can also meditate on devotion, in order to understand and increase it; or on impermanence, where one contemplates an object and the way in which it is constantly changing; or on emptiness, realizing that the object has no true existence.

There are many ways to describe the perception of things. In meditation it is important to be able to distinguish between the perceived object, the object in itself, the object as it is considered to be, and the object of intention.[35] We should also study the five defects to be avoided in mental calm meditation, mentioned in the *Treatise on the Center and Extremes*.[36]

In brief, meditation is a way of training and transforming the mind, and this it certainly does. For our purposes, the main thing is to develop the one-pointed concentration of mental calm and to meditate on bodhichitta. For concentration to become clear, we need the right conditions, namely, freedom from outer distractions. The ideal is to meditate in a secluded place that is conducive to physical and mental serenity.

> 3. On account of loved ones and desire for gain,
> Disgust with worldly life does not arise.
> These are, then, the first things to renounce.
> Such are the reflections of a prudent man.

4. The penetrating insight of a mind that calmly rests
   Destroys completely all afflicted states.
   Knowing this, one must begin by searching for
     tranquility,
   Found by those who turn with joy their backs upon
     the world.

7. If for other beings there is craving,
   A veil is cast upon the perfect truth,
   Wholesome disillusion melts away,
   And finally there comes the sting of pain.

8. My thoughts are all for them,
   And by degrees my life is frittered by.
   My family and friends will fade and pass,
   And yet for them the changeless doctrine is forsaken.

As we are impermanent, is it really worth being so attached to
others, who are also impermanent? Is it really worth getting angry
with them? Let us reflect on this and stop the stream of clinging and
aversion.

9. If I act like those who are like children,
   Sure it is that I shall fall to lower states.
   Why then keep the company of infants
   And be led by them in ways so far from virtue?

Ordinary beings dominated by gross attachment and hatred are
like children. If we behave like them, we will not achieve anything
for ourselves, and it will be impossible for us to benefit them. One
minute they are our friends, the next they turn against us. However
hard we try, it is difficult to please them. And when we do not listen
to them, they become angry.

13. Associate with childish ones—what follows?
    Self-praise, putting others down, and
    Chattering about the pleasures of saṃsāra.
    Every kind of vice is sure to come.

14. This kind of link between myself and others
    Will be productive only of misfortune:
    They will bring no benefit to me;
    Neither shall I do them any good.

It is therefore better to keep our distance from such beings. In doing so, however, we should avoid offending them, and when we do meet them, we should be courteous and do what we can to make them happy, without becoming too familiar.

16. Like bees that get their honey from the flowers,
    Take only what is consonant with Dharma.
    Treat them like first-time acquaintances;
    Do not be familiar with them.

Let us not be attached to ephemeral pleasures. It is only ignorant and confused people who spend their time amassing possessions. They end up with suffering a thousand times as great as the happiness they seek.

19. This being so, the wise man does not crave,
    Because from craving fear is born.
    And fix this firmly in your understanding:
    All that may be wished for will fade naturally to nothing.

20. For though they get themselves a wealth of property,
    Enjoying reputation, sweet celebrity,
    Who can say where they have gone to now,
    With all the baggage of their affluence and fame?

What point is there in hoping for people's approval and fearing their criticism? If a few people sing our praises, there is not much to be happy about, because there might be many more who are secretly criticizing us. We need not worry when a few criticize us, because there are others who have only praise for us. The wants and needs of others are so various that it is impossible for us ordinary beings to satisfy them all. Even the Buddhas themselves cannot do so. So it is better to distance ourselves from the childish and consider instead the advantages of living in solitude.

> 25. In woodlands, haunt of stag and bird,
> Among the trees where no sounds jar upon the ear,
> Such would be my pleasant company.
> When might I go and make my dwelling there?

> 26. When will I live and make my home
> In cave or empty shrine or under spreading tree,
> And have within my breast a free, unfettered heart,
> Which never turns to cast a backward glance?

In such secluded places we can give up attachment to our belongings and bodies and devote all our time to meditation.

> 28. When might I be free of fear,
> Without the need to hide from anyone,
> With just a begging bowl and few belongings,
> Dressed in garments coveted by nobody?

> 33. Like those who journey on the road,
> Who halt and make a pause along the way,
> Beings on the pathways of the world,
> Halt and pause and take their birth.

> 34. Until the time comes round when
> Four men carry me away,

Amid the tears and sighs of worldly folk—
Till then, I will away and go into the forest.

35. There, with no befriending or begrudging,
I will stay alone, in solitude,
Considered from the outset as already dead,
Thus, when I die, a source of pain to none.

In short, in lonely places one is able to meditate with one-pointed concentration, free from personal concerns and attachment. Thoughts of the Buddha and his teachings come naturally to mind.

Shāntideva continues by pointing out the mistake of being attached to sensual pleasures. As the *Bodhicharyāvatara* was originally addressed to a community of monks, this section deals especially with the defects of the female body, but it should be understood that a woman practitioner can apply the same method of reflection to men's bodies.

40. Sending messengers and go-betweens
With many invitations to the bride,
Avoiding, in the quest, no sin
Or deed that brings an evil name,

41. Nor acts of frightful risk,
Nor loss and ruin of their goods and wealth.
And all for pleasure and the perfect bliss,
That utmost penetrating kiss

42. Of what in truth is nothing but a heap of bones,
Devoid of self, without its own existence!
If this is all the object of desire and lust,
Why not pass beyond all pain and grief?

Think about it: the person to whom we are so attracted, and for whom we have undergone so many ordeals, is only a mass of flesh and organs and rather unpleasant substances. What is it then that we are attached to—the person's body or mind? If we check carefully, we find that we cannot point at any real thing that is the source of our attachment.

54. "But it is the skin and flesh I love
    To touch and look upon."
    Why then do you not wish for flesh alone,
    Inanimate and in its natural state?

55. The mind of the one you love so much
    Eludes your touch; this mind you cannot see.
    Everything that sense perceives is not the mind,
    Therefore, why indulge in pointless copulation?

Let us examine the body. First of all, it originates from the procreative fluids of the parents. Once mature, it is made up of blood, flesh, organs, and bones. Were we to find any one of these things left on the ground, we would be utterly revolted. Why then are we not repelled by the body, which is wholly made up of disgusting elements?

63. Thus the unclean nature of such things
    Is manifest, and yet if even now I harbor doubts,
    Then I should go to charnel grounds
    And look upon the fetid carrion.

A large part of what we eat and drink to sustain this body ends up as an unending stream of urine and excrement, filling the sewers we find so offensive. But the very reason there are sewers is that our bodies are full of excrement. The body is no different from a sewer! As we have seen, it originates from filth, consists of filth, and churns out filth. Only when we think about the body from this point of view, says the *Garland of Jewels,* will our attachment to the body begin to diminish, if not entirely disappear.

Again, take someone with a very beautiful body. Suppose the skin were removed and the body opened up. Even in a living person, the internal organs are a gruesome sight. Our desire would soon give way to revulsion. Attachment to the body is illusion on top of illusion, and we should do our best to undo it.

> 70. Did you see the heaps of human bones
> And feel revulsion in the charnel ground?
> Then why such pleasure in your cities of the dead,
> Filled with animated skeletons?

We experience endless difficulties trying to find the ideal partner, and once we have done so, we do not always get on well together. We cannot have children, or we have too many, and bringing them up adds to our problems. Of course, in the beginning the novelty is enjoyable, but if we examine things closely, we find that suffering just follows on suffering. This is why the sūtras refer to "the malady of household life."

As for wealth, we go to great lengths to obtain it, and are even prepared to lose our lives for it. Once we have it, we are forever afraid of losing it. Because of wealth, brothers and sisters are set at odds, couples break up. When we do not have it we suffer; when we have it we also suffer!

> 79. The suffering of guarding what we have, the pain of
>   losing all—
> We should see the endless troubles brought on us by
>   wealth.
> Those distracted by their love of property
> Will never have a moment's freedom from the
>   sorrows of existence.

80. Those indeed possessed of many wants
    Suffer many hardships, all for very little—
    Mouthfuls of the hay the oxen get,
    Their fine reward for having pulled the cart!

For the smallest of pleasures, people waste their human lives that have cost them a disproportionately greater effort to obtain.

82. All that we desire is sure to perish,
    And then into infernal pain we fall.
    The constant little hardships and fatigue
    We undergo, and all for no great matter—

83. With a millionth part of such vexation
    Buddhahood itself can be attained!
    The pains the lustful take exceed by far the troubles
    Of the path of freedom and will give no freedom at
        the end.

So we should examine the things that excite our distracted thoughts. Gradually these thoughts will become less strong, and our minds will become more calm. Then we will be able to meditate one-pointedly on bodhichitta.

The main meditation on bodhichitta consists of considering oneself and others to be equal and then exchanging oneself with others. As Shāntideva says:

The mighty Buddhas, pondering for many kalpas,
Have seen that this and only this will save
The boundless multitudes of beings
And bring them easily to supreme joy! [chap. 1, v. 7]

The masters of the Kadampa tradition left detailed teachings on different ways of practicing bodhichitta. By generating bodhi-

96

chitta through such practices, we can purify all our obscurations and accumulate positive actions. It is said that we have to accumulate merit over three uncountable kalpas, but these terms are relative. With the attitude of bodhichitta such enormous amounts of merit are quickly and easily achieved. All the learned and accomplished masters, from the Buddha through Nāgārjuna and his disciples down to our own present teachers, took the practice of considering others more important than themselves as the foundation of their own practice. Through this they were able to benefit themselves and others on a vast scale.

Anyone who has good thoughts, who does a lot to help others, and who leaves behind good memories is respected by people all over the world, regardless of whether they are religious or not. On the other hand, the ignorance, arrogance, and obstinacy of certain individuals, whether their intentions were good or evil, have been at the root of all the tragedies of history. The mere names of these ruthless tyrants inspire fear and loathing. So the extent to which people will like us naturally depends on how much or how little we think of others' good.

Speaking of my own experience, I sometimes wonder why a lot of people like me. When I think about it, I cannot find in myself any specially good quality, except for one small thing. That is the positive mind, which I try to explain to others and which I do my best to develop myself. Or course, there are moments when I do get angry, but in the depth of my heart, I do not hold a grudge against anyone. I cannot pretend that I am really able to practice bodhichitta, but it does give me tremendous inspiration. Deep inside me, I realize how valuable and beneficial it is, that is all. And I try as much as possible to consider others to be more important than myself. I think that's why people take note of me and like me, because of my good heart.

When people say that I have worked a lot for peace, I feel embarrassed. I feel like laughing. I don't think I have done very much for world peace. It's just that my practice is the peaceful path of kindness, love, compassion, and not harming others. This has become part of me. It is not something for which I have specially volunteered. I am simply a follower of the Buddha, and the Buddha taught that patience is the supreme means for transcending suffering. He said, "If a monk harms others, he is not a monk." I am a Buddhist monk, so I try to practice accordingly. When people think this practice is something unique and special and call me a leader of world peace, I feel almost ashamed!

A good heart is the source of all happiness and joy, and we can all be good-hearted if we make an effort. But better still is to have bodhichitta, which is a good heart imbued with wisdom. It is the strong desire to attain enlightenment in order to deliver all beings from suffering and bring them to Buddhahood. This thought of helping others is rooted in compassion, which grows from a feeling of gratitude and love for beings, who are afflicted by suffering.

Traditionally there are two methods for developing this sort of care and gratitude. One is to reflect on the fact that all beings have at some time in the succession of their lives been our parents, or at least close friends, so that we naturally feel grateful to them and wish to take on their suffering in exchange for our happiness. The other method is to understand that others suffer in the same way as we do, to see that we are all equal, and to reflect on what is wrong with egotism and on the advantages of altruism. We can use whichever of these two methods suits us best or practice them both together.

In either case, it is necessary first to understand what we call suffering. It is easy enough for us to feel compassion for people who are starving, in pain, or in great distress and for animals who are maltreated. But when we think of human and celestial beings who are very happy, we tend to feel envious. This is because we have not really understood what suffering is and that all beings suffer. Apart from the more obvious torments of *suffering added to suffering* and *suffering of change*, there is *all-pervading suffering*.[37] Because of the latter, as long as we are in saṃsāra, we can never have lasting happiness. Once we have reflected on and understood this for ourselves, we can apply this understanding to others. Then we start to feel compassion and think, I must free all these beings from suffering.

However, to actually do so, we have to change our approach to this life and to our future lives. First we must reflect on impermanence, on the certainty of our own death, and on the fact that we can never know how soon we might die. After death, we will not simply vanish: the positive and negative actions we have done will determine how we are reborn. Our negative actions might cause us to be reborn in the lower realms, for example as animals—exploited, maltreated, and butchered by humans or devoured by other animals.

So to free ourselves from the ocean of suffering, we should begin to study and practice the path of liberation. We might hope to see some result after a few years, but speaking realistically, we should plan on probably having to continue our practice over many lives to come. In each of these lives we are going to need a proper support for practice, namely, a human body, without which it will be impossible to make progress. The first stage on the path, therefore, is to ensure a good human rebirth. So although our final aim is to achieve enlightenment for all beings, we have to begin the path by following the discipline of avoiding the ten nonvirtuous actions and practicing the ten virtuous actions.

To summarize, we start by getting rid of our attachment to nonspiritual goals, first in this life and then in future lives. Having seen the suffering inherent in saṃsāra, we resolve to free ourselves, and as we extend this attitude to other beings, we develop compassion and generate bodhichitta. We have to go through these stages of training the mind in the right order, like going up some stairs or like building the foundation before we build a wall. If we follow the path gradually in this way, the result we have will be stable. But if we simply say, "For the sake of all beings . . ." however strong our wish to help beings might be at that moment, it will not be stable unless it is well founded on the correct practice of the earlier stages.

In the beginning we should have a clear, overall view of the path, so that we know what we are aiming at in our practice and can recognize the level we have reached. Then, as we practice regularly, we may experience profound changes in our minds, but these experiences only occur when we are concentrating in sessions of meditation. Later, after meditating for a long time, we find that these experiences occur spontaneously when we encounter particular circumstances, without our needing to concentrate in meditation.

Take the example of bodhichitta. After we have meditated on bodhichitta for a while, a change occurs in our minds, but only when we are actually thinking of bodhichitta. This is what is called a fabricated experience. It is not the bodhichitta of a real Bodhisattva. As we maintain progress, however, we reach a point where the mere sight of an animal or bird causes the thought to well up from the depth of our hearts, When will I ever attain enlightenment for this being? This is what we call a natural experience, and at this point true bodhichitta has taken root in us. We can genuinely call ourselves practitioners of the Mahāyāna and are then on the lesser path of accumulation.

Proceeding on the middle path of accumulation, we then begin the greater path of accumulation of merit, which lasts three uncountable kalpas. This is followed by the path of connection with its four stages of warmth, climax, endurance, and supreme realization. Then as we start on the path of seeing, we gain the wisdom of the first Bodhisattva level. In this way, we gradually traverse the five paths and ten levels and ultimately attain Buddhahood.[38] These paths and levels are therefore related to our own inner transformation through the practice of bodhichitta.

90. Strive at first to meditate
 Upon the sameness of yourself and others;

In joy and sorrow all are equal.
Be the guard of all, as of yourself.

In what way are others equal to us? Just like us, they naturally want to be happy and to avoid suffering. Although on analysis we are unable to find an "I" that truly exists, we are still convinced that it does exist, and we therefore consider that we have a right to be happy and a right to escape unhappiness. But this is also the case for all other beings, so there is no particular reason why we should be any more important than them. Why should we accomplish only our own happiness and not be responsible for others' happiness? Why should we make an effort to avoid suffering for ourselves and not be responsible for doing the same for others?

When we try to protect our bodies, we also protect the parts of the body, such as our hands and feet. Similarly, since the happiness and suffering of others are all part of the same happiness and suffering that is ours, we must protect others from suffering just as much as we protect ourselves and strive for others' happiness just as we do for our own.

Our own sufferings, though not felt by others, are certainly hard for us to bear. So it is natural that we should try to protect ourselves from suffering. Similarly, others' pain, even if we do not feel it, is no less unbearable for them. But as we are related to all other beings, as we owe them our gratitude and they help us in our practice, let us try to dispel their suffering as well as ours. All beings equally want to be happy, so why should we be the only ones to get happiness? Why should we be protected from suffering and others not be?

94. So I will dispel the pain of others,
    Since pain it is, just like my own.
    And others I will aid and benefit,
    For they are living beings, just like me.

101

97. —Since the pains of others do no harm to me,
    Why protect and make a guard against them?
    —But why to guard against "my" future pain, which
    Does no harm to this, my present "me"?

One might think that one has to protect oneself from future suffering because the "I" that suffers now and the "I" that will suffer in the future are the same. This is wrong, because what we think of as "I" is a succession of instants in a continuum of consciousness, and the "I" of the moment that will suffer in future is different from the "I" of the present moment.

99. It is surely for the sufferer himself
    To parry any injury that comes!
    The pain felt in my feet is not my hand's;
    Why then does my hand protect my foot?

If one were to think that everyone should take care of his or her own suffering, one could argue that the hand should protect only itself and no other part of the body: there is no reason why the hand should protect the foot. Although we might find this argument convenient, it is not at all logical. Let us stop being stubborn and thinking only of ourselves.

101. Labeled continuities and aggregates,
     Such as strings of beads and armies, are deceptive;
     Likewise, there is none who has the pain.
     Who is there to be oppressed by it?

102. But if there is no subject suffering,
     There can be no difference in the pain of self and
         other.
     Simply, then, since pain is pain, I will dispel it.
     What use is there in making such distinctions?

When we talk about "I" and "beings," these are not independent entities. They are false labels applied to a continuum of impermanent elements, just as "necklace" is applied to a string of beads or "army" to a collection of soldiers. However, if beings have no real existence, who is in pain? Why try to dispel suffering? Although the "I" does not truly exist, in relative truth everyone wants to avoid suffering. This is sufficient reason for dispelling the sufferings of others as well as our own. What is the use in discriminating?

> 103. Thus, the suffering of everyone
> Should be dispelled, and here there's no debate.
> To free myself from pain means freeing all;
> Contrariwise, I suffer with the pain of beings.

We might think, If I meditate on compassion and think of the suffering of others, it will only add to the intense pain I already have. We only think like this because we are narrow-minded. If we do not want to help beings, then their suffering will be endless. But if we can develop a little compassion and make an effort to dispel the suffering of others, then that suffering will have an end. Without our taking the responsibility to help others, there can be no limit to suffering. When we develop a broad mind and feel compassion for others, this is vastly beneficial. Any small difficulties we might experience are worthwhile.

> 105. If through such a single pain
> A multitude of sorrows can be remedied,
> Such pain as this all loving ones
> Should strive to foster in themselves and others.

The great Bodhisattvas are prepared to do anything, even lose their lives, if it will eradicate the misery of numerous other beings.

> 107. Those whose minds are practiced in this way,
> Whose happiness it is to soothe the pain of others,

Will venture in the hell of unremitting agony
As swans sweep down upon a lotus lake.

108. The oceanlike immensity of joy
Arising when all beings are set free—
Is this not enough? Does this not satisfy?
The wish for my own freedom, what is it to me?

For a Bodhisattva who wears the armor of determination, the joy he has from alleviating the pain of infinite beings is sufficient on its own, even if he suffers a little himself. How could achieving liberation for ourselves alone, while abandoning our promise to liberate others, be better than that?

109. The work of bringing benefit to beings
Will not, then, make me proud and self-admiring.
The happiness of others is itself my satisfaction;
I will not expect some ripening reward.

Let us never think, If I help others, I will accumulate positive actions. I will be a virtuous person and in the future I'll be happy. This is not the point. Let us do positive actions with profound compassion to relieve others' unhappiness, and let us dedicate these actions to their well-being, from the depth of our hearts, without the slightest notion of future personal reward.

We shall now discuss the exchange of self and others. This practice consists of putting ourselves in the place of others and putting others in our own place. If we train in this, we come to consider others more important than ourselves, so that their happiness and suffering become more important than ours, and when they are harmed, we feel it as acutely as when we ourselves are harmed. This is not difficult to do once we have realized the disadvantages of thinking only of ourselves and the benefits of cherishing others. Our exchange of self and others becomes so vivid and strong that it is easy for us to give our lives for others. And by others we mean all beings everywhere.

> 114. Just as hands and other limbs
> Are thought of as the body's members,
> Shall I not consider other beings
> As the limbs and members of a living body?

We should not be deterred by the difficulty of such a practice. It is a question of getting used to it through training. For example, it is possible to become used to a person whose mere name once made one afraid. One can even reach the point where one cannot bear to be separated from that person.

> 120. Those who desire speedily to be
> A refuge for themselves and other beings,
> Should take the place of others, giving them their
> own,
> Undertaking thus a sacred mystery.

This sure method for protecting others, including oneself, is nevertheless difficult for those with a limited understanding of bodhichitta. This is why Shāntideva refers to it as a "sacred mystery." As he points out, the principal obstacle is cherishing oneself:

> 121. Because of our attachment to our bodies,
> We are terrified by only little things.
> This body, then, the source of so much fear—
> Who would not revile it as the worst of enemies?

> 122. Wishing to relieve our bodies' wants,
> Our hungry mouths, the dryness of our throats,

We lie in wait along the road
And steal the lives of fishes, birds, and deer.

123. For their bodies' service and advantage
There are those who even kill their fathers or their
mothers
Or steal what has been offered to the Triple Gem,
Because of which they will be burned in deepest hell.

To sustain this body of ours, to which we are so attached, we kill other beings. To make it comfortable, we steal. To satisfy its ephemeral desires, we indulge in indiscriminate sexual activity. In short, because of the importance we attribute to our bodies, we accumulate a lot of negative actions. If we let our bodies do whatever they want, it can only be to our loss and detriment.

124. Where then is the prudent man
Who wants to pamper and protect his body,
Who does not disregard and treat with scorn
What is for him a dangerous enemy?

125. "If I give this, what is left for me?"
Thinking of oneself—this is the path of evil ghosts.
"If I keep this, what is left to give?"
Concern for others is the way of gods.

If we harm and impoverish others to further our own interests, we shall be reborn in lower realms, such as the hells. On the other hand, if we forget ourselves in order to benefit others, if we are prepared to give our own lives to save the lives of others, giving them whatever is necessary for their welfare, then we shall gain happiness and all perfection.

The result of wishing to be superior to others, to be famous, will be lower rebirth or rebirth as an idiot, in abject misery, with an ugly body. On the other hand, true humility, treating others as more important than ourselves, will lead to our being reborn in the higher realms, where we will be respected and influential. If we force others to work for us and serve us, inconsiderately abuse them, in future rebirths we shall end up as their servants or even their servants' servants. Whereas if it is we who spend our lives serving others, we shall be reborn as kings and leaders.

These, then, are the benefits to be gained from regarding others as more important than oneself and the disadvantages of giving oneself precedence.

> 129. All the joy the world contains
> Came through wishing happiness for others;
> All the misery the world contains
> Came through wanting pleasure for oneself.

> 130. Is there need for lengthy explanation?
> Childish beings look out for themselves;
> Buddhas labor for the good of others.
> See the difference that divides them!

> 131. If I do not give away
> My happiness for others' pain,
> Buddhahood will never be attained,
> And even in saṃsāra, joy will fly from me.

Our greatest enemy is to consider ourselves more important than others, which leads us and others to certain ruin. From this attachment to "I" arises all the harm, fear, and suffering in this world. What, asks Shāntideva, am I to do with this great demon?

> 135. If there is no self-surrender,
> Sorrow likewise cannot be avoided.

A man will not escape from being burned
If he does not keep away from fire.

136. To free yourself from harm
And others from their sufferings,
Give away yourself for others,
Holding others dear as now you do yourself.

137. "For I am now beneath the power of all,"
This, O mind, must be your certainty;
Now no longer shall you entertain a thought
But to contrive the benefit of beings.

138. My sight and other senses, now the property of
others—
To use them for myself would be illicit.
How much more so is it disallowed to use
My faculties against their rightful owners.

As we have taken the vow to devote ourselves solely to helping
other beings and from the depths of our hearts have given everything
to them, we should consider that our bodies are no longer ours but
belong now to them. So we must never use any part of our bodies to
do anything that does not help others. Whatever we can see in ourselves that is good, let us snatch it away from ourselves and use it to
serve others.

We come now to a practice that is special to the *Bodhicharyāvatara:*

140. Think of lesser beings as yourself,
And identify yourself with others,
Then, your mind relieved of scruples,
Cultivate a sense of envy, pride, and rivalry.

Here we begin by evaluating our own good and bad qualities and, on this basis, comparing ourselves with others, distinguishing between those who are equal to us, those who are superior, and those who are inferior. To do this we make a distinction between our new, good side—which has seen what is wrong with considering ourselves more important than others and the benefits of regarding others as more important than ourselves—and our old, bad side, the egotistic "I." The new "I" now identifies itself with other beings and takes their side. The old "I" has three aspects: superior, equal, and inferior. And the new "I," which is now identified with others, has these three aspects as well. We shall use these two distinct "I's" to develop successively a sense of jealousy, competition, and pride.

First, we look at the good qualities in which we surpass others. Identifying ourselves (our new "I") with these inferior beings, we make ourselves jealous of the superior qualities of the old, egotistic "I." It is not fair, we cry, that he is respected while we are not!

141. "He is the center of attention; I am nothing!
     I am poor without possessions, unlike him;
     Everyone looks up to him, despising me;
     All is well for him; for me there's only bitterness.

142. "All I have is sweat and drudgery,
     While there he's sitting at his ease.
     He is great, respected in the world;
     I'm an underdog, a well-known nobody."

If we find this comparison too humbling, we should not get discouraged at our lack of good qualities. Let us remember that all beings possess the potential for enlightenment and that we can attain Buddhahood if we make the effort. There is no reason, therefore, to be discouraged.

143. "What! A nobody without distinction?
Not true! I do have some good qualities.
He's not the best, he's lower down than some,
While, compared to some, I'm excellent!"

It is not our fault that we are inferior but the fault of the negative emotions. These notions of superiority and inferiority are entirely relative. We tell the old "I": You are only superior because I am inferior, so if you want to stay superior, you will have to put up with me while I strive for enlightenment. What use are your good qualities if they don't benefit me? In this way, when we see qualities in ourselves that make us better than others, we should exchange roles and destroy our feelings of superiority.

Next we take those who are our equals, and again siding with them, we develop a sense of competition with our old "I," thinking only of getting the better of him and making him miserable.

148. "I will noise abroad by every means
My qualities to all the world,
Ensuring that whatever qualities he has
Remain unknown to anyone.

149. "My faults I will conceal.
I, not he, will be the object of devotion;
I, not he, will gain possessions and renown;
I will be the center of attention.

150. "I for long will look with satisfaction
On his humiliation and disgrace;
I will render him despicable,
The mock and laughingstock of all.

Finally, we think of those aspects in which we are inferior to others, and then looking at our old "I" through others' eyes, we develop a sense of pride.

151. "The rumor is that this unhappy wretch
     Is trying to compete with me!
     How could he be like me in intelligence,
     In learning, beauty, wealth, or pedigree?

152. "Oh, the pleasure, sending shivers
     Up my spine, I have and revel in
     To hear that everyone is talking
     Of how talented I am!

153. "Well then, even if he does have something,
     I'm the one he's working for!
     He can have enough to live on;
     I'm the boss, though, and the rest is mine!

154. "I will wear his happiness away;
     I will always hurt and injure him.
     He's the one who in saṃsāra
     Did me mischiefs by the thousand!"

Putting ourselves in the place of others is very helpful for seeing the faults of the egotistic "I," and we become deeply disgusted with it. When we practice like this, using jealousy as a tool, let us imagine that our old "I" is very good-looking, well-dressed, wealthy, powerful, and has everything he needs. Then we imagine ourselves as an impartial spectator in the midst of a crowd of paupers, dressed in rags, the lowest of the low. Now observe the old "I," who since time without beginning has thought only of himself and has never given a thought for others. To further his own interests, he has enslaved others and has not hesitated to kill, steal, lie, slander, and selfishly indulge in sex. He has been nothing but a burden on others' lives. When we look at the egotistic "I" in this way, true disgust will well up in our hearts. And as we identify ourselves with these other beings, in all their misery, we will feel closer to them, and the wish to help them will grow.

We should make our practice on competitiveness and pride equally vivid and real. Let us remind ourselves of all the negative actions the "I" has made us do, all the harm it has done us, making us suffer and causing endless suffering for others, too. This is our real enemy. Would it not be wonderful to make it suffer more than we do, or even make it disappear altogether? Should we not be genuinely proud if we could break it and render it powerless?

> 156. The truth, therefore, is this:
> You must wholly give yourself for others.
> The Buddha did not lie in what he said;
> The benefits therefrom are later sure to come.

Having examined all that is wrong with considering ourselves more important than others, and having seen all the harm such an attitude brings, we should revolt against its domination and never let the thought of our own importance influence us.

> 170. Every thought of working for myself
> Is now rejected, cast aside.
> "Now you have been sold to others,
> Stop your whining, be of service!"

> 171. For if, through being inattentive,
> I do not deliver you to others,
> You will hand me over, this is certain,
> To the guardians of hell.

> 173. It is thus: If I wish for happiness,
> I should never seek to please myself.
> So it is that if I wish to save myself
> I must always be the guardian of others.

Shāntideva stresses particularly the dangers of being attached to one's body.

174. As much as this my human form
     Is cosseted and guarded,
     Indeed to that extent
     It grows so sensitive and peevish.

175. And one who falls to such a state,
     The earth in its entirety
     Is powerless to satisfy.
     Who can therefore give him all he craves?

Attachment to the body can only bring us suffering. If we cherish it because it is useful to us, then we should regard everyone else's bodies in the same way, because their bodies are useful to them.

184. Therefore, free from all attachment,
     I will give this body for the benefit of beings;
     Thus, though many blemishes afflict it,
     I shall take it as my necessary tool.

Until now, we have let ourselves be dominated by our clinging to "I." It is high time we put a stop to this childish behavior by following in the footsteps of the Bodhisattvas, recalling the instructions on carefulness, and warding off dullness and sleep. Like those compassionate Heirs of the Conquerors, we should patiently practice day and night. If we can do that, it is certain our suffering will one day come to an end.

187. Thus, to banish all obscuring veils,
     I shall turn my mind from the mistaken path,
     And constantly upon the perfect object
     I shall rest my mind in even meditation.

9

Wisdom

1. All these branches of the Doctrine
The Powerful Lord expounded for the sake of wisdom.
Therefore, they must generate this wisdom
Who wish to have an end of suffering.

THERE ARE many kinds of wisdom. There is, for example, the relative type of wisdom gained through the study of the five major traditional sciences.[39] There is also the wisdom of working for the benefit of others. When Shāntideva says here that "all these branches of the Doctrine were expounded for the sake of wisdom," he is referring to the wisdom that is the realization of emptiness, the true nature of things. This is absolute wisdom.

In order to realize emptiness, we do not actually need the first five pāramitās, and they are not even essential for developing clear insight for vipashyanā. But as we shall see, they are necessary if we wish to benefit other beings.

Nāgārjuna says in the *Seventy Verses on Emptiness:*

Thus the Buddha said:
All things arise from causes and conditions;
To view them as real is ignorance
From this arise the twelve interdependent links.[40]

Further, it is said in the *Four Hundred Verses:*

The seed of existence is consciousness;
Phenomena are the field of consciousness.

If we see the nonreality of things,
We destroy the seed of existence.

These passages can be interpreted in various ways, but according to the tradition of Chandrakīrti, which is the one to which Shāntideva adhered, the teaching of Nāgārjuna and his lineage says that to cling to the self as a real entity is to be ignorant, and the ignorance of believing that phenomena truly exist constitutes one of the twelve interdependent links. This gives rise to saṃsāric existence, which in turn is another of the twelve interdependent links.

The second passage states that the seed of this saṃsāric existence is the kind of consciousness that has objects, or phenomena, as its field of experience. If these objects are understood to be devoid of ultimate reality, this seed of existence is undermined, and it is completely destroyed when the wisdom of realizing that phenomena are without true existence is perfectly developed.

All schools of Buddhism, with one minor exception, agree that the notion of a personal self, the "I," is dependent upon the five aggregates. They reject the belief in a self that exists independently of these aggregates. The theory of selflessness, however, goes much further than the denial of the personal "I." For one must aim to realize that all phenomena are empty, or devoid of true existence, and have in fact a mode of being that is extremely subtle.

As we have said, when we see that phenomena or objects of consciousness are devoid of any true entity, the seed of existence is destroyed. The reverse of this understanding is to cling to the belief that things have a solid reality, and this is the definition of ignorance.

It is a mistake to believe that those who practice the lower vehicles are unable to free themselves from negative emotions and thereby attain liberation from saṃsāra. Indeed, to think like this is a major breach of the Bodhisattva precepts. When those who follow the paths of the Shrāvakas and Pratyekabuddhas become Arhats,[41] they completely rid themselves of the obscurations engendered by negative emotions. They must also have a realization of emptiness, otherwise they would not be freed from saṃsāra. The wisdom of understanding emptiness in fact gives rise to three types of enlightenment: that of the Shrāvakas, that of the Pratyekabuddhas, and that of the Bodhisattvas.

When Shāntideva says, "All these branches of the Doctrine/ The Powerful Lord expounded for the sake of wisdom," he is referring to the wisdom of the Bodhisattvas and not to the mere insight into emptiness cultivated by the Shrāvakas and Pratyekabuddhas as they progress upon their respective paths. What, then, is special about the Bodhisattvas' wisdom? Why do they meditate on emptiness? Bodhisattvas aim to rid themselves not only of the obscurations created by negative emotions but also of the obscurations that are obstacles to knowledge. They must free themselves from the former before they can deal with the latter.

Nevertheless, it may be said that in certain circumstances negative emotions provide the occasion for a good result, as when the cherishing of others arises through desire. As the proverb says, "Foul sewage from the city of Serkya fertilizes the fields of sugarcane." In fact, however, the Bodhisattvas' real enemies, and the greatest hindrances in their work for others, are the obscurations that veil omniscience. But since these consist in the residual traces left by negative emotions, it follows that the latter must be abandoned before the obstacles to knowledge can be removed.

Thus, when Bodhisattvas meditate on emptiness, their aim is mainly to dispel these obstacles to knowledge. In order to do this, it is not enough simply to have an intellectual understanding of the subtle nature of things. The wisdom that dispels these obscurations must be supported by such practices as generosity and the other pāramitās.[42] The Buddha taught these different practices so that Bodhisattvas could attain the clear insight through which they might dispel obstacles to knowledge and then work for the benefit of others.

In talking about generating wisdom to put an end to suffering, Shāntideva is referring to the suffering of *all* beings. After all, this text is about the activities of the Bodhisattva, and have we not only recently discussed what is wrong with cherishing oneself and why it is important to think of others?

When generosity and so forth are practiced as pāramitās, are practiced with an understanding that the subject, object, and the action itself are all devoid of true existence, these acts become very profound and completely transcend ordinary generosity and so on.

We should note that Shāntideva talks about generosity first and places the topic of wisdom only at the end. He had a reason for this. In the *Compendium of All Practices*, just before beginning his exposition of emptiness, he shows with numerous quotations from the sūtras that the Buddha himself, before broaching the same subject, would speak about the unattractiveness and impermanence of phenomena and about the nature of suffering. One might almost think that the world of phenomena was the main subject of his teaching, for it was only in conclusion that he would say that things have no true, objective existence. There was, however, an extremely important reason for his proceeding in this way. To begin with, he would discuss the positive and negative aspects of things, laying the ground for a clear understanding of the unfailing functioning of relative truth, according to which things do indeed exist. It was on the basis of their relative existence that the Buddha explained that phenomena are empty by their nature. Only where there is a basis is it possible to assert emptiness. As it is said: "Form is emptiness; emptiness is form." Because there is form, we can talk about its nonexistence. If there were no form, there could not be emptiness of form. As there are phenomena that we can talk about as being empty, we say there is a basis for emptiness. Without that basis, emptiness would be inconceivable.

An explanation of the practices of the first five pāramitās, starting with generosity, gives us a clear view of the basis for emptiness.

When, for example, we practice generosity to remove for ourselves and others all suffering due to poverty, we are cognizant of the relative truth of cause and effect. When it is subsequently explained that, in absolute truth, all this is actually devoid of real existence, we are already firmly grounded in relative truth and are thus protected from erring into the philosophical extremes of nihilism or eternalism.

2. Conventional and ultimate—
    These the two truths are declared to be.
    The ultimate is not within the scope of intellect,
    For intellect is said to be conventional.

A distinction is made, with regard to knowable things, between the relative (conventional) and the absolute (ultimate) truth. According to the root text, absolute truth cannot be perceived by the intellect.

As we find in the *Prajñāpāramitā:*

The pāramitā of wisdom is inconceivable, inexpressible, and
    indescribable.
It is not born; it does not cease; it is like space.
Only the awakened mind can comprehend it.
Before the Mother of all the Buddhas, I bow down!

Again, the *Vajra Cutter Sūtra* says:

The absolute nature of the Buddhas,
The absolute body of the spiritual guides,
Cannot be understood by the intellect.

The reason for this, as Shāntideva says, is that the intellect is something that exists on the level of relative truth. However, the interpretation of this point is delicate, because later in the text we shall read about another kind of intellect and intelligence. Shāntideva continues:

3. Two kinds of people are to be distinguished:
   Meditative thinkers and ordinary folk.
   The concepts of the ordinary give way,
   Refuted by the views of meditators.

4. And within the ranks of these philosophers,
   The lower in degrees of insight are confuted by the
      higher.
   Comparisons are held in common;
   In order to achieve the goal, analysis is left aside.

When the text speaks about insight or intelligence, it is referring to the understanding of lack of true existence. In the use of discriminating wisdom to analyze phenomena, the different schools gain different levels of this understanding, and those with more advanced philosophical views confute those with less advanced views.

Again, there are two kinds of discriminating wisdom. One discriminates things concerning relative truth, and the other discriminates things concerning absolute truth. Here in the text, insight, or intelligence, refers to discriminating wisdom that analyzes the absolute nature of things and not intelligence in its more general sense concerning relative phenomena. And if the verse is considered in terms of the profound path and the vast path, it is the profound path that is referred to.

It is said in the *Entrance to the Middle Way:* "One who is at the level *further to go* has superior intelligence." When a Bodhisattva reaches the seventh level, which is called *further to go*, his intelligence surpasses that of a Shrāvaka or Pratyekabuddha. Until then, Bodhisattvas on the first level upward surpass the Shrāvakas and Pratyekabuddhas because of their *family*, not because of the power of their intelligence, or their understanding of emptiness.[43] Only when they reach the seventh level is their intelligence superior. It is also said that at this point they surpass the Shrāvakas and Pratyekabuddhas in their ability, in a single instant, to enter into and arise from the concentration of perfect cessation.

When Shāntideva says that absolute truth cannot be perceived by intellect, he is referring not to the intelligence that discerns absolute truth but to the obscured intelligence that conceives the dichotomy of subject and object. Absolute truth is something that we have to experience with a mind free of concepts and in which there are no such dualistic notions. Relative truth is what is perceived by the conceptual, dualistic intelligence.

The non-Buddhist traditions of ancient India also talked about absolute and relative truths. The Sāṃkhyas, for example, regarded the primal substance as absolute truth, and the rest of the twenty-five objects of knowledge (such as the Self) as relative truth. Even between the different Buddhist schools—the Vaibhāshika, Sautrāntika, Chittamātrin and Mādhyamika—the two truths are explained in slightly different ways.

The term *relative* is sometimes called an obscuring truth and sometimes a conventional truth, depending on the context. And *absolute truth* can also have many different meanings. The *Treatise on the Center and Extremes* speaks of absolute absolute truth, practiced absolute truth, and attained absolute truth. Again, in the supreme Mantrayāna one speaks of the absolute luminosity. Moreover, to explain the specific practices of the Mantrayāna, the two truths are explained in different ways. For example, the illusory and temporary aspect of phenomena is related to relative truth, while their aspect of primordial continuity is related to absolute truth.

So when we talk about the absolute truth, we should always do so with reference to the context, whether Sūtrayāna or Mantrayāna, and if Mantrayāna, to the particular tantra. We should then gain a precise understanding of absolute truth within that context. This is very important. If we try to apply only a general understanding of absolute truth to some specific text, we can get very confused.

It is said in the *Root Verses of the Middle Way* that the teachings of the Buddha rely on the two truths: the truth of the relative world and the supreme, absolute truth. This is explained in detail in the *Entrance to the Middle Way*, which says that, as all phenomena are perceived both correctly and mistakenly, we apprehend their nature in two ways. What is correctly perceived is absolute truth, and what is perceived incorrectly is relative truth. This refers to the findings of nonconceptual experience, related to absolute truth, and those of conceptual analysis, related to relative truth. It is on the basis of these that we establish our understanding of emptiness. But here we are only talking about the nonconceptual experience of the absolute truth. With this exception, the ways of distinguishing the truths are the same as in the *Entrance to the Middle Way*.

Why do we need to realize emptiness? We do not wish to suffer, and we know that the root of suffering is the untamed mind. Because the mind perceives and understands things mistakenly, negative emotions arise and the mind is never at peace. This is why we suffer. To avoid this, we must develop the unmistaken mind, the intelligence that perceives the true nature of phenomena. Mistaken perception arises because we fail to see things as they are.

Much of what we perceive we perceive in a mistaken way, seeing things not as they truly are. This is how we become deluded. To avoid this, we should not accept our perceptions just as we experience them. It is very important to analyze and investigate whether we are seeing things as they truly are. We should ask ourselves what our perceptions are masking. If we do this, an understanding of the two truths will arise in our minds.

All we perceive—mountains, houses, and so on—affect us in one way or another. We need to investigate their real nature. Our perceptions, and the positive and negative aspects that we attribute to them, constitute relative truth. Relative truth is what we find when we experience the multiplicity of phenomena in a relative way, without going any further in analyzing their nature. The findings of the analysis by the conventional mind constitute relative truth.

If, according to absolute truth, things have no true existence, why do we speak of relative truth as *truth?* Because it is true for the perceiver. It is true for the mind clouded by ignorance, which believes in the reality of its perceptions. As the *Entrance to the Middle Way* says, that which is altered and obscured by ignorance and is perceived as real is called relative truth.

For which mind is the multiplicity of phenomena true? It can only be the confused ignorant mind that believes that things exist objectively. The true nature of things is obscured by the mind's ignorant clinging to things and to the way they function. Thus, relative truth is based on the findings of the mind that examines things in a conventional way. If we analyze further and try to see the true nature of phenomena, we can find the ultimate nature of reality. Here we distinguish between the way things appear (relative truth) and the way they are (absolute truth), which is what is perceived by the undeluded mind.

There are two ways of approaching absolute truth: a positive idea of it can be gained through listening, reflecting, and meditating, and an understanding of it in terms of negation can be gained by analysis. It stands to reason that if one can find through analysis anything that truly exists one should also be able to find it through listening, reflecting, and meditating. But the fact is, what one can find through listening, reflecting, and meditating cannot be found by analysis. The absolute nature, for example, is something that can be experienced through listening, reflecting, and meditating. When one investigates the nature of the individual and of all phenomena, one finds that their nature is emptiness. This emptiness is an absolute truth that is apparent to the mind. One can see it with one's awareness. Once it has been experienced, it is not necessary to demonstrate it again. By referring to one's experience of this nature one can recall it. Its existence is true, and one does not have to rely on argument to prove that it exists. So when one has some confidence that no phenomena truly exist, one does not need to have this explained again or to repeat the investigation. This absolute nature that is established through listening, reflecting, and meditating is something we can experience.

However, when one looks for this absolute nature or emptiness, and tries to find where it is, one cannot find it. Its nature is nonexistent. When one makes the absolute nature (that one experienced through listening, reflecting, and meditating) the object of analysis, one cannot find it. This is why it is called nonexistent by nature. To take an example, we can say that a vase has the nature of emptiness, but when we look for that emptiness, it is nonexistent. All we can find is the emptiness of emptiness, but we cannot find emptiness. What has been found by experiencing it through listening, reflecting, and meditating cannot be found through such analysis.

This is an important point. The understanding of absolute truth that comes from listening, reflecting, and meditating is something that exists and can be experienced. But in the absolute truth that appears through the analysis even of emptiness itself, there is nothing that exists.

10

Dedication

THE FINAL CHAPTER of the *Bodhicharyāvatara* is the dedication of merit for the benefit of all beings.

1. By whatever virtue I have here accrued
   From the making of this song,
   This guide for entry on the Bodhisattva way,
   May everyone begin to tread the path to Buddhahood.

2. Beings everywhere, tormented
   By the sufferings of mind and body,
   May they gain, by virtue of my merit,
   Joy and happiness in boundless measure.

3. As long as they may linger in saṃsāra,
   May their joy know no decline,
   And in uninterrupted stream
   May they taste of unsurpassed beatitude.

On this last day I would like to thank you all for coming so far to attend these teachings. I would like to have given a more detailed commentary on the ninth chapter, the wisdom chapter, but there has not been enough time. However, this provides a good reason for coming back to France, and I am determined to return so that we can spend a week studying only the ninth chapter.[44]

All of you here, spiritual friends with a genuine interest in the teachings of Buddha, please study and practice as much as you can.

The basic knowledge and understanding you have gained on the subject of emptiness will make your practice much easier. This understanding of emptiness will be much more powerful if it is founded on the practice of altruism. As Shāntideva wrote the *Bodhicharyāvatara* primarily as a manual for practitioners, rather than as a theoretical treatise, we should do our best to apply these teachings on unselfishness. Living for others is of immense importance for all of us, whatever our beliefs.

We are all here on this planet, as it were, as tourists. None of us can live here forever. The longest we might live is a hundred years. So while we are here we should try to have a good heart and to make something positive and useful of our lives. Whether we live just a few years or a whole century, it would be truly regrettable and sad if we were to spend that time aggravating the problems that afflict other people, animals, and the environment. The most important thing is to be a good human being.

I have noticed some old friends here among you, Western Buddhist monks and nuns who have been practicing and keeping vows of ordination for more than fifteen years, some as long as twenty years. You are almost elders of the Sangha! I've noticed from your posture and gaze that while you are listening to the teachings you are fully concentrated on the subject. This is very pleasing, and I hope you will continue so that you achieve genuine bodhichitta and the realization of emptiness. This is possible through inner transformation. One day you will become Bodhisattvas in reality. So whatever obstacles there are, however long it takes, do not get discouraged. And in the meanwhile, I would like to thank you very much.

Here in Dordogne there are Nyingma and Kagyu Buddhist centers, and elsewhere in France, there are Gelug and Sakya centers. I am very pleased to see that these different traditions maintain a strong spirit of harmony among themselves, with no sectarian prejudice. Please continue to cultivate this spirit.

I would like to say a few words concerning the Tibetan cause.

As a Buddhist monk, I do not find any difficulty in being involved in this national struggle, because it is related to the Buddhadharma and is not merely a political question. Without freedom, the Buddha's teachings cannot be practiced and preserved. The last thirty years have proved this. A free Tibet is therefore very important for the preservation of these teachings, especially so since Buddhism has been practiced in Tibet in a very complete form. Helping this cause will indirectly serve the Buddhadharma. Some of you here are actively defending the rights of Tibetans. I very much appreciate this and ask you to continue your support. I would like to thank you deeply on behalf of all those who live under constant fear and threat and in the name of more than one million Tibetans who have disappeared as a result of this tragedy.

55. And now, as long as space endures,
    As long as there are beings to be found,
    May I continue likewise to remain
    To soothe the sufferings of those who live.

56. The pains and sorrows of all wanderers—
    May they ripen wholly on myself.
    And may the virtuous company of Bodhisattvas
    Ever bring about the happiness of beings.

57. May the Doctrine, only remedy for suffering,
    The source of every bliss and happiness,
    Be nurtured and upheld with reverence
    And throughout a vast continuance of time endure!

    May precious bodhichitta take its birth
    In those in whom it has not taken birth.
    And where it has been born, let it not cease,
    But swell and increase ever more and more.

NOTES

1. Kunu Rinpoche (1885–1977), who was originally from India, studied in Tibet and became one of the Dalai Lama's teachers.
2. Patrul Rinpoche (1808–1887) was an outstanding teacher from Kham in eastern Tibet. He was recognized as an emanation of Shāntideva and of Chenrezi, the Buddha of Compassion. He is perhaps best known for his book, *Kunzang lame shelung* (translated as *The Words of My Perfect Teacher*, forthcoming 1994 from ISLT / Harper San Francisco).
3. Shāntideva was an eighth-century Buddhist master at the monastic university of Nālandā in India. It was to the monks of Nālandā that he first taught the *Bodhicharyāvatara.*
4. The *Heart Sūtra* is the most concise form of the Prajñāpāramitā Sūtras and contains the essence of the teachings on emptiness. The *Praise to Mañjushrī (Shrī-jñānagunabhadranamastuti)* is a prayer to the Buddha of Wisdom, often recited before studying a Buddhist text. A mandala, a symbolic representation of the universe, is offered to the teacher along with the request to give the teachings.
5. The Wheel of Dharma is the symbol of the Buddha's teaching. Turning the Wheel of Dharma is synonymous with expounding the teachings. Further explanation is given later in this chapter.
6. Vinaya is the section of the Buddha's teachings that deals with moral conduct, in particular the vows and precepts for ordained monks and nuns and the Buddhist laity.
7. A lineage is a line of Buddhist teachers who transmit to their spiritual heirs the teachings they have themselves received and inherited from their own teachers. A lineage can be related to one particular text or to a group of teachings. Most lineages can be traced back ultimately to the Buddha himself. The Dalai Lama's lineage for the *Bodhicharyāvatara* runs from Shāntideva through a continuous line of Buddhist masters to Patrul Rinpoche, then to Khenpo Shenga (1871–1927), Kunu Rinpoche, and the Dalai Lama himself.
8. Minyak Kunzang Sonam was a great Gelug scholar who studied under Patrul Rinpoche for almost twenty years. His commentary on the *Bodhicharyāvatara* is the most detailed one available.
9. Jamyang Khyentse Wangpo (1820–1892) was responsible for a Buddhist renais-

sance in Tibet in the last century. This great lama was one of the founders of the Rime, or nonsectarian, movement.

10. In Mahāyāna Buddhism, the term *lack of self* (Tib. *bdag med;* Skt. *nairātmya*) applies not only to the individual's ego but to all phenomena, *self* meaning in this context real or substantial entity. A Bodhisattva has to realize the lack of self in him- or herself as an individual and in all other phenomena.

11. First level: see Glossary, *Ten levels*

12. The ten pāramitās consist of the *six pāramitās* (see Glossary) together with skillful means, strength, aspiration, and primordial wisdom.

13. Nāgārjuna (first or second century) was an Indian master responsible for the propagation of the prajñāpāramitā teachings. His teachings on emptiness formed the basis for the Mādhyamika doctrine, or Middle Way.

14. See Glossary, the *Eighteen characteristics of a precious human existence.*

15. Gendun Drubpa (1391–1474) was first in the line of reincarnations who subsequently (during the life of the third) received the title Dalai Lama. He is thus the "first" Dalai Lama.

16. Āryadeva (second century) continued the work of Nāgārjuna and further explained the teachings of the Middle Way.

17. See chap. 8, page 98, for a traditional method of developing compassion and concern for other beings by regarding them as one's parents.

18. The Seven Branch Prayer is a practice for purifying oneself and accumulating merit through homage, making offerings, confession, rejoicing in others' virtue, requesting teachings, entreating the Buddhas and other teachers to remain in this world, and dedicating one's merit to the enlightenment of all beings.

19. Abhidharma is the section of the Buddha's teachings that explains Buddhist metaphysics and the various levels on the path to Buddhahood.

20. The term *demon* is often used in Buddhism to denote any obstacle to spiritual progress. Such obstacles are manifestations of our own minds and karma. They should not be thought of as hostile, animate beings threatening us from outside.

21. Dignāga was a fifth- to sixth-century Indian master.

22. The sixteen subdivisions of the Four Noble Truths are (1) the truth of suffering: suffering, impermanence, emptiness, and lack of true reality; (2) the truth of the origin of suffering: origin of suffering, production, causal basis, and conditions; (3) the truth of cessation: cessation, pacification, excellence, and renunciation; (4) the truth of the path: path, knowledge, accomplishment, and liberation.

23. The eight close disciples are the eight Bodhisattvas: Mañjushrī, Avalokitesh-

vara, Vajrapāṇi, Ākāshagarbha, Kshitigarbha, Sarvanivāraṇavishkambhin, Maitreya, and Samantabhadra.

24. The six ornaments are Nāgārjuna, Āryadeva, Asaṅga, Vasubandhu, Dignāga, and Dharmakīrti.

25. The two supreme teachers are Shāntideva and Chandragomin.

26. An example of this would be telling a lie if to do so will save the life of someone.

27. The three poisons are hatred, attachment, and ignorance.

28. The rūpakāya is the *form* body of a Buddha, in which he appears to beings. It comprises the *sambhogakāya* and the *nirmānakāya* (see Glossary).

29. For example, the merit gained through the meditation of a celestial being (deva) in the realm of formlessness cannot be destroyed by anger arising in the human state.

30. A Pure Land is a world manifested by a Buddha or Bodhisattva in accord with the merit of sentient beings. Beings reborn in a Pure Land are able to progress swiftly on the path to Buddhahood.

31. Details of the Sāṃkhya doctrine can be found in T. R. V. Murti, *The Central Philosophy of Buddhism* (London: Allen and Unwin, 1960).

32. Escape from a supposedly permanent saṃsāra is a contradiction in terms.

33. The realm of nothing at all is one of the four formless worlds, or realms, at the summit of cyclic existence, experienced through the four formless absorptions said to be attained by practitioners of the Brahma Vehicle. Beings in these worlds have temporarily suppressed the gross negative emotions but their minds are still pervaded by ignorance and they lack any realization of selflessness. For this reason they cannot escape from saṃsāra and continue to take rebirth in the lower realms. See Glossary, *Three worlds.*

34. The Mādhyamika view is the view of the Middle Way introduced by Nāgārjuna. It is discussed more fully in chapter 9 of the *Bodhicharyāvatara.*

35. These are four ways of perceiving an object. See Anne C. Klein, *Knowledge and Liberation* (Ithaca, N.Y.: Snow Lion, 1986), pp. 108–110.

36. The five defects that interrupt mental calm are laziness, forgetting the instructions on meditation, dullness and being distracted by thoughts of attachment, lack of effort, and overexertion. See *Mahamudra*, trans. Lobsang P. Lhalungpa (Boston: Shambhala Publications, 1986), p. 21.

37. The three sufferings are as follows: (1) *Suffering added to suffering* is what all beings can perceive as undesirable and painful; in saṃsāra, sufferings follow each other in endless succession. For example, when one is already stricken with illness, one succumbs to another malady, or the loss of all one's possessions is followed

by one's house being burnt down. (2) *Suffering of change* refers to the fact that any happiness and pleasure in saṃsāra is bound to change, sooner or later, into a state of suffering. For example, the gustative pleasure experienced during a delicious meal may give way to the discomfort of indigestion. (3) *All-pervading suffering* has been defined as suffering resulting from the very fact of having the five skandhas, or aggregates. As long as one takes conditioned existence in saṃsāra, there is suffering. Most ordinary beings are unable to perceive this clearly, just as one might not feel a hair on the palm of one's hand. But in the same way as a hair in the eye causes intense irritation and pain, realized beings experience this all-pervading suffering acutely. Further explanation is to be found in Gampopa's *The Jewel Ornament of Liberation,* trans. H. V. Guenther (Boston: Shambhala Publications, 1986) and in Patrul Rinpoche's *The Words of My Perfect Teacher.* (See note 2.)

38. The *five paths* and *ten levels*: see Glossary.

39. The five major sciences are languages, logic, crafts, medicine, and philosophy.

40. See Glossary, *Twelve links of interdependence.*

41. Arhat means "one who has destroyed the enemies." The enemies referred to are the negative emotions, which are vanquished through the practice of the teachings of the fundamental vehicle, or Shrāvakayāna. Arhats achieve liberation from the sufferings of saṃsāra, but because their realization of emptiness is not perfect, they are unable to remove the subtle veils of attachment to phenomenal reality, which are the obstacles to omniscience. They have yet to enter the Mahāyāna in order to progress towards the supreme goal of Buddhahood.

42. This is because the mind must be supported and strengthened by an enormous stock of merit in order to be able to realize emptiness.

43. Because the Shrāvakas and Pratyekabuddhas seek liberation only for themselves, they are considered to be of inferior *family* to those who belong to the Bodhisattva family and strive for the enlightenment of all beings.

44. His Holiness did indeed teach the ninth chapter of the *Bodhicharyāvatara* to a large audience in November 1993 at the Institut Vajrayogini, Lavaur. A translation of his commentary is in the course of preparation. He based his teaching on two detailed commentaries by Khenpo Kunzang Palden and Minyak Kunzang Sonam (see note 8). These two commentaries have been translated, at his express wish, under the title *Wisdom: Two Buddhist Commentaries,* translated by the Padmakara Translation Group (Peyzac-le-Moustier, France: Padmakara, 1993).

GLOSSARY

Bodhichitta   The mind of enlightenment. This is a key word in the Mahāyāna. On the relative level, it is the wish to attain Buddhahood for the sake of all beings and the practice necessary to do this. On the absolute level, it is the direct insight into the ultimate nature of self and phenomena.

Bodhisattva   A practitioner on the path to Buddhahood, training in the practice of compassion and the six pāramitās (q.v.), who has vowed to attain enlightenment for the sake of all beings. The Tibetan translation of this term means "hero of the enlightened mind."

Bodhisattvayāna   The vehicle of the Bodhisattvas within the Sūtrayāna (q.v.) or the Sūtrayāna part of the Mahāyāna.

Buddha   One who has removed the two veils (the veil of afflictive emotions, which is the cause of suffering, and the veil of ignorance, which is the obstacle to omniscience) and who has brought to perfection the two sorts of knowledge (of the ultimate and relative nature of phenomena).

Buddhadharma   The teaching of the Buddha. *See also* Dharma.

Circumambulation   A highly meritorious devotional practice, consisting in walking clockwise, concentratedly and with awareness, around a sacred object, such as a temple, stupa, holy mountain, or the house—and even the person—of a spiritual master.

Clear, or penetrating, insight (Skt., *vipashyanā*)   Meditation that reveals the absence of inherent existence in both the mind and phenomena.

Dharma   The body of teaching expounded by Shākyamuni Buddha and other enlightened beings that shows the way to enlightenment. It comprises two aspects: the Dharma of transmission, namely, the teachings that are actually given, and the Dharma of realization, or the states that are attained through the application of the teachings.

Dharmakāya   The absolute, or truth, body; an aspect of emptiness.

Doctrine   *See* Dharma.

Eight worldly preoccupations   Gain or loss, pleasure or pain, praise or criticism, and fame or infamy. Most people who are not following a spiritual path seek gain and try to avoid loss, and so on for each of these pairs of opposites.

Eighteen characteristics of a precious human existence   These eighteen characteristics comprise eight freedoms and ten endowments. The eight freedoms consist in not being born (1) in the realms of hell; (2) as a hungry ghost; (3) as an animal; (4) in the realms of the gods; (5) among barbarians who are ignorant of the teachings and practices of the Buddhadharma; (6) as one with wrong views, such as those of nihilism, of the substantiality of the ego and phenomena, etc.; (7) in a time or place where a Buddha has not appeared; and (8) as mentally handicapped. The ten endowments are subdivided into five that are considered intrinsic and five considered extrinsic. The five intrinsic endowments are (1) to be born as a human being; (2) to inhabit a *central land*, that is, one where the Buddhadharma is proclaimed; (3) to be in possession of normal faculties; (4) to be one who has not abandoned oneself to great karmic negativity; and (5) to have faith in the Dharma. The five extrinsic endowments are the facts (1) that a Buddha has appeared in the world; (2) that he has expounded the Dharma; (3) that his Teaching still persists; (4) that it is practiced; and (5) that one is accepted as a disciple by a spiritual master.

Five aggregates (Skt., *skandhas*) The five psychophysical constituents that characterize sentient beings: form, feeling, appraisal, impulse, and consciousness.

Five paths The paths of accumulation, preparation, seeing, meditation, and no more learning. These represent successive stages in spiritual progress rather than distinct and different pathways to enlightenment. A Bodhisattva on the path of no more learning has attained Buddhahood. *See also* Ten levels.

Five poisons The five principal negative emotions: ignorance, attachment, hatred, pride, and jealousy.

Four Noble Truths (1) Suffering: the nature of existence in saṃsāra is suffering. (2) Cause: the cause of suffering is negative or obscuring emotions. (3) Cessation: the cessation of suffering is Buddhahood. (4) Path: the path is the means to attain liberation.

Fundamental Vehicle *See* Shrāvakayāna.

Gelug One of the four main traditions of Tibetan Buddhism, founded by Tsongkhapa (1357–1419).

Higher realms *See* Six realms.

Hīnayāna *See* Shrāvakayāna.

Kadam Lineage of Tibetan Buddhism deriving from the teachings of Atīsha (982–1054). Its teaching emphasizes monastic discipline, study, and the practice of compassion. The influence of the Kadam tradition is pervasive in all schools of Tibetan Buddhism, although it is especially associated with the Gelug teaching, which is indeed sometimes referred to as the New Kadam.

Kagyu   One of the four main traditions of Tibetan Buddhism, founded by Marpa the Translator (1012–1095).

Kalpa   An immense period of time as conceived in the traditional cosmology of India. A great kalpa, which corresponds to the period of formation, duration, disappearance, and absence of a universal system, comprises eighty small kalpas. An intermediary kalpa consists of two small kalpas taken together, in the first of which the duration of life increases, while in the second it decreases.

Karma   Sanskrit word meaning "action," understood as the law of causality. According to the Buddha's teaching, all actions, whether of thought, word, or deed, are like seeds that will eventually bear fruit in experience, whether in this or future lives. A positive or virtuous act will result in happiness, and the definition of sin or negative action is that which is the cause of suffering later on.

Lower realms   *See* Six realms.

Mahāyāna   The Great Vehicle, including the teachings of both Sūtrayāna and Mantrāyana (q.v.). *See under* Shrāvakayāna.

Mantra   A group of words or syllables associated with specific meditational deities, the recitation of which forms an essential part of tantric meditation.

Mantrayāna   The vehicle of the secret mantras, sometimes called the Diamond Vehicle, or Vajrayāna. This collection of teachings and practices is based on the tantras, and though it is, in fact, an aspect of the Mahāyāna, it is sometimes considered a separate vehicle. *See* Shrāvakayāna.

Mental calm (Skt., *shamatha*)   A state in meditation in which the mind concentrates one-pointedly and effortlessly on the object of meditation.

Negative emotions or afflictions (Skt., *klesha*)   Mental factors whose influence on thoughts and actions ultimately produces suffering. The five principal negative emotions are the five poisons (q.v.).

Nirmānakāya   The manifestation body, the aspect of compassion and means, whereby a Buddha may be perceived by unenlightened beings. This is, therefore, the means by which he can communicate with and help them.

Nirvāṇa   The Tibetan translation of this Sanskrit word means "gone beyond suffering" and indicates the various levels of enlightenment gained according to the practice of the Shrāvakayāna or the Mahāyāna.

Nyingma   The earliest of the four main traditions of Tibetan Buddhism, founded in the eighth century by Guru Padmasambhava.

Pratyekabuddha   One who attains enlightenment alone, without the aid of a master, and who does not transmit teachings to others.

Refuge   A Buddhist seeks the protection and guidance of the Three Jewels (q.v.)

in order to find freedom from the suffering of saṃsāra. The Three Jewels therefore constitute the Buddhist refuge, and a Buddhist can be defined as someone who *takes refuge* in them.

Sambhogakāya   The body of enjoyment, or the transhuman forms in which Buddhas may manifest themselves. The sambhogakāya is directly perceptible only to highly realized beings.

Saṃsāra   The wheel, or round, of existence. The state of being unenlightened, in which the mind, enslaved by the three poisons of attachment, hatred, and ignorance, passes uncontrolled from one state to another through an endless stream of psychophysical experiences that are all characterized by suffering. *See also* Six realms; Three worlds.

Sakya   One of the four main traditions of Tibetan Buddhism, founded by Khon Konchok Gyalpo (1034–1102).

Shrāvakayāna or Hīnayāna   The practitioners of Dharma are identified as belonging to two different sets of teaching, or *vehicles*, according to the nature of their aspirations. These are known as the Hīnayāna, or Fundamental Vehicle, and the Mahāyāna, or Great Vehicle. The Fundamental Vehicle is subdivided into the way of the Hearers (or Shrāvakas), who are disciples of the Buddha, and the way of those who seek enlightenment relying only on themselves, or Pratyekabuddhas. The goal of the Shrāvaka and Pratyekabuddha paths is nirvāṇa, conceived of as definitive liberation from the sufferings of saṃsāra. The Great Vehicle is that of the Bodhisattvas, or those who, while accepting the validity and efficacy of the other vehicle, aspire to the full enlightenment of Buddhahood for the sake of all beings. The term *Hīnayāna* means "Lesser Vehicle," but this should not be understood in a pejorative sense, since its teachings are fundamental to the practice of the Great Vehicle as well. The Dalai Lama has suggested the term *Shrāvakayāna* be used instead of Hīnayāna. In this case the term should be understood as including the Pratyekabuddhayāna as well.

Six pāramitās, or transcendent practices   The six activities of generosity, moral discipline, patience, endeavor, meditative concentration, and wisdom, which form the practice of the Bodhisattva path. They are termed transcendent because, unlike ordinary generosity, etc., they are untainted by attachment and other negative emotions.

Six realms   The experience of beings in saṃsāra is traditionally schematized into six general categories, referred to as realms or worlds, in which the mind abides as the result of previous actions, or karma. None of these states is satisfactory, though the degree of suffering in them differs from one to another. The three higher, or fortunate, realms, where suffering is alleviated by temporary pleasures, are the heavens of the celestial beings, or devas; the realms of the Āsuras, or demigods; and the world of human beings. The three lower realms, in which suffering predominates over every other experience, are those of the animals, the hungry ghosts, and the hells.

Sūtras   The teachings given by Shākyamuni Buddha, memorized by his disciples, and subsequently written down.

Sūtrayāna   The Mahāyāna has two subsections: the Sūtrayāna, that is, the teachings based on the sūtras and propounding the practice of the six pāramitās, and the Mantrayāna, the teachings and practices based on the tantra texts.

Tathāgata   An epithet for a Buddha.

Tathāgatagarbha   The Buddha nature, the potential for Buddhahood, present in the mind of every sentient being.

Ten levels   Stages on the path to enlightenment. The first Bodhisattva level marks the beginning of the path of seeing. The second to tenth levels are progressive stages within the path of meditation.

Three Jewels or Triple Jewel   The Buddha, the Dharma (Doctrine), and the Sangha (Assembly of disciples and practitioners). These are the three objects of refuge.

Three trainings   Discipline, concentration, and wisdom.

Three worlds, or realms   In some contexts samsāra is spoken of as being divided into three worlds, or realms—those of desire, of form, and of formlessness. The world of desire includes all the six realms (q.v.). The worlds of form and formlessness exist only for certain types of celestial beings, who have attained these states through the four meditative concentrations of form and the four formless absorptions, respectively.

Triple Gem   *See* Three Jewels.

Twelve links of interdependence   Ignorance, habitual tendencies, consciousness, name and form, the six sense fields, contact, feeling, craving, grasping, coming into being (existence), birth, and old age and death.

Vajrayāna   *See* Mantrayāna.

BIBLIOGRAPHY

Bodhisattva Levels: *Bodhisattvabhūmi* by Asaṇga (fourth century).

Compendium of All Practices: *Shiksasamuccaya* by Shāntideva (eighth century).

Compendium of All Sūtras: *Sūtrasamuccaya* by Shāntideva.

Compendium of Logic: *Pramana-samuccaya-nama-prakarana* by Dignāga (fifth–sixth centuries).

Entrance to the Middle Way: *Mādhyamaka-āvatara-nama* by Chandrakīrti (seventh century).

Essence of the Middle Way: *Mādhyamaka-hridaya-kārikā* by Bhāvaviveka (sixth century).

Four Hundred Verses: *Catuhshataka-shāstra-kārikā* by Āryadeva (second century).

Garland of Jewels: *Ratnamala* by Chandraharipa.

General Counsels: *Udanavarga.*

Heart Sūtra: *Prajñāpāramitā-hridaya-sūtra.*

Ornament of the Mahāyāna Sūtras: *Mahāyāna-sūtralamkāra-kārikā* by Maitreya-Asaṇga.

Root Verses of the Middle Way: *Prajñā-mūlamādhyamaka-kārikā* by Nāgārjuna.

Seventy Verses on Emptiness: *Shūnyatāsaptati-kārikā* by Nāgārjuna.

Stories of the Buddha's Series of Lives: *Jatakamala* by Aryashura.

Sublime Continuum: *Uttaratantra-shāstra* by Maitreya-Asanga.

Sūtra of Buddha Nature: *Tathāgatagarbha-sūtra.*

Sūtra of the Three Collections: *Triskandha-sūtra.*

Sūtra of the Vajra Banner: *Vajradhvaja-sūtra,* part of the *Avatamsaka Sūtra.*

Sūtra of the Visit to Lankara: *Lankāvatāra-sūtra.*

Sūtra of Transcendent Wisdom: *Prajñāpāramitā-sūtra.*

Treatise on Logic: *Pramanavarttika-kārikā* by Dharmakīrti (seventh century).

Treatise on the Center and Extremes: *Mādhyanta-vibhanga-kārikā* by Maitreya-Asanga.

Vajra Cutter Sūtra: *Vajracchedikā-sūtra.*

Way of the Bodhisattva: *Bodhicharyāvatara* by Shāntideva.

INDEX

Abhidharma, 23, 128n.19
Activity, 2
Aggregates, 4, 115, 132
    demon of the, 25
Anger, 52–55, 57–59, 63–66, 70–71
Arhat, 115, 130n.41
Āryadeva, 20, 128n.16
Attachment, 39, 92, 99
    antidote to, 4
    to the body, 45, 113
    to "I," 107
    to sensual pleasures, 93–95

Bodhicharyāvatara, viii–xii, 9, 16, 50
    original audience of, 93
    special practice of, 108
    structure, 16
    transmission, 1
Bodhichitta, 2, 12, 16–18, 34, 36, 57, 74,
        98, 100, 131
    application, 19, 31–32
    aspiration, 19, 31–32
    benefits, 16
    definition, 12, 131
    generation of, 30, 31
    meditation on, 96
    vow of, 19
Bodhisattva, 9, 11, 19, 82, 84, 100, 103,
        104, 119, 125
    activities, 80
    definition, 12
    discipline, 40, 65
    precepts, 115

    training of, 11
    vow, 12
Bodhisattva Levels, 50
Bodhisattvas,
    Vehicle of 27. *See also* Bodhisattva-
        yāna
Bodhisattvayāna, 131
Buddha, 2, 9, 11, 25–27, 32, 49, 97, 117,
        131
    Children of, 11, 18, 35
    Sons of, 9, 11, 113

Chandrakirti, 115
Chittamātrin, 29, 120
Clear insight, 7, 21, 88, 90, 114, 116, 131
Compendium of All Practices, 49, 50, 117
Compendium of All Sutras, 51
Compendium of Logic, 26
Confession, 24

Dalai Lama, vii–xii
    first, 128n.15
Death, 24–25, 76–77, 99
    demon of, 25
Dedication of merit, 31, 71, 124
    prayer of, 1
Desire. *See* Attachment
Dharmakāya, 10, 11, 131
Dignāga, 26, 128n.21
Discouragement, 80

Eight worldly preoccupations, 23, 69, 131
Emotions,
    negative, 1, 5, 14, 20, 35–38, 57, 66, 76,
        133

negative, demon of, 25
negative, root of, 20
Emptiness, 2, 12, 89, 114, 117, 122, 123
Enlightenment, three types of, 116
Entrance to the Middle Way, 23, 53, 119, 121, 122
Essence of the Middle Way, 15

Five major sciences, 114, 130n.39
Five Paths, 100, 132
Four Hundred Verses, 114
Four Noble Truths, 4–6, 132
    sixteen subdivisions, 27, 128n.22

Garland of Jewels, 81, 95
Gendun Drubpa, 19, 128n.15
Generosity, 7, 16, 19, 52, 70, 117, 118
    of protecting from danger, 43
Good heart, 97, 98, 125

Hatred, 52, 54–55, 57, 63
    antidote to, 4
Heart Sutra, 2, 127n.4
Human life, 18, 20, 45, 77, 131–132

Ignorance, 4, 13, 115, 122
    antidote to, 4
Impermanence, 1, 27, 89, 99, 117
Interdependence, 2, 3, 4, 60, 63, 79
    twelve interdependent links, 114–115, 135

Jamyang Khyentse Wangpo, 8, 127n.9
Jealousy, 30, 67, 69, 109, 111
Joy, 47, 104
    in doing good, 76
    as a support for endeavour, 84

Karma, 3, 18, 23, 81, 133
    common, 23
    law of, 4

Kunu Rinpoche, 1, 7, 127n.1

Laziness, 76–80
Levels,
    first, 10, 100, 119
    seventh, 119, 120
Love, 4, 58, 79, 98

Mādhyamika, 29, 88, 120, 129n.34
Mahāyāna, 7, 12, 133
Mañjushrī, Praise to, 2, 127n.4
Mantrayāna, 40, 88, 133
Mental calm, 7, 21, 88, 89, 133
Mental calm meditation,
    five defects to be avoided, 89
Minyak Kunzang Sonam, 8, 17, 127n.8

Nāgārjuna, 13, 20, 51, 97, 114, 115, 128n.13
Nirmānakāya, 11, 133
Nirvāna, 15, 31, 49, 72, 133

Ornament of the Mahāyāna Sūtras, 50
Ornaments, six. *See* Six Ornaments

Pāramitās. *See* Six pāramitās
Path,
    of accumulation, 100
    of application, 100
    of no more learning, 11
    of seeing, 100
Patience, 52–74
Patrul Rinpoche, 1, 17, 127n.2
Poisons,
    five, 132
    three, 43
Prājñapāramitā, 12, 118
Prajñāpāramitā Sūtra, 2, 127n.4
Prakriti, 60
Pratyekabuddha, 11, 27, 115, 116, 119, 133

Pride, 24, 83, 110
  antidote to, 4
  demon of, 25
Primal substance, 60
Puruṣha, 60

Rahula, 11
Rebirth, 23, 77–78, 106
Refuge, 2, 11, 24–27, 133
Rejoicing, 30, 47, 67
Root Verses of the Middle Way, 121
Rūpakāya, 46, 129n.28

Sambhogakāya, 11, 134
Sāṃkhyas, 59, 60, 61, 120, 129n.31
Samsāra, 15, 61, 99, 134
  root of, 13
Sautrāntika, 29, 120
Sciences, five major. *See* Five major sciences
Self-confidence, 24, 82, 83. *See also* Pride
Seven Branch Prayer, 21, 32, 128n.18
Seventy Verses on Emptiness, 114
Shamatha, 7, 88. *See also* Mental Calm
Shāntideva, viii–xii, 1, 127n.3
Shrāvaka, 11, 27, 115, 116, 119
Shrāvakayāna, 6, 7, 134
Six Ornaments, 32, 129n.24
Six pāramitās, 7, 11, 12, 16, 114, 117, 134
Skandhas. *See* Aggregates
Specific Counsels, 50
Stories of the Buddha's Series of Lives, 50
Sublime Continuum, 5, 14
Suffering, three kinds of, 98, 129n.37
Sugata, 9, 10
Supreme teachers, two. *See* Two supreme teachers
Sutra in Three Sections, 49

Sutra of Buddha Nature, 5
Sutra of Interdependence, 61
Sutra of the Vajra Banner, 82
Sutra of the Visit to Lankara, 27

Ten Levels, 100, 135
Ten pāramitās, 11, 128n.12
Three Jewels, 2, 11, 24, 135
Three Trainings, 7, 135
Treatise on Logic, 9, 28
Treatise on the Centre and Extremes, 89, 120
Truth,
  absolute, 118–123
  relative, 103, 117–122
Truths
  Four Noble. *See* Four Noble Truths
  two, 118–121
Two supreme teachers, 32, 129n.25

Vaibhāshika, 29, 120
Vajra Cutter Sutra, 118
Vajrayāna, 7, 135
Vehicle,
  Fundamental, 6, 134
  Great, 7, 133
View, 2
Vinaya, 6, 40, 43, 127n.6
Vipashyanā, 7, 88, 114. *See also* Clear insight

Wheel of Dharma, 2, 127n.5
  first turning, 4
  request to turn, 31
  second turning, 5, 12
  third turning, 5
  three turnings, 4, 8
Wisdom, 5, 11, 114–123
Worldly preoccupations. *See* Eight worldly preoccupations

SHAMBHALA DRAGON EDITIONS

The Art of War, by Sun Tzu. Translated by Thomas Cleary.

The Awakened One: A Life of the Buddha, by Sherab Chödzin Kohn.

Bodhisattva of Compassion: The Mystical Tradition of Kuan Yin, by John Blofeld.

The Book of Five Rings, by Miyamoto Musashi. Translated by Thomas Cleary.

The Buddhist I Ching, translated by Thomas Cleary.

Cutting Through Spiritual Materialism, by Chögyam Trungpa.

Dakini Teachings: Padmasambhava's Oral Instructions to Lady Tsogyal, by Padmasambhava. Translated by Erik Pema Kunsang.

The Diamond Sutra and The Sutra of Hui-neng. Translated by A. F. Price & Wong Mou-lam. Forewords by W. Y. Evans-Wentz & Christmas Humphreys.

The Essential Teachings of Zen Master Hakuin, translated by Norman Waddell.

The Experience of Insight: A Simple and Direct Guide to Buddhist Meditation, by Joseph Goldstein.

A Flash of Lightning in the Dark of Night: A Guide to the Bodhisattva's Way of Life, by Tenzin Gyatso, the Fourteenth Dalai Lama.

Great Swan: Meetings with Ramakrishna, by Lex Hixon.

I Am Wind, You Are Fire: The Life and Work of Rumi, by Annemarie Schimmel.

Insight Meditation: The Practice of Freedom, by Joseph Goldstein.

Living at the Source: Yoga Teachings of Vivekananda, by Swami Vivekananda.

Living with Kundalini: The Autobiography of Gopi Krishna.

The Lotus-Born: The Life Story of Padmasambhava, by Yeshe Tsogyal.

Mastering the Art of War, by Zhuge Liang & Liu Ji. Translated & edited by Thomas Cleary.

The Myth of Freedom and the Way of Meditation, by Chögyam Trungpa.

Nine-Headed Dragon River, by Peter Matthiessen.

Returning to Silence: Zen Practice in Daily Life, by Dainin Katagiri, Foreword by Robert Thurman.

Seeking the Heart of Wisdom: The Path of Insight Meditation, by Joseph Goldstein & Jack Kornfield. Foreword by H. H. the Dalai Lama.

Shambhala: The Sacred Path of the Warrior, by Chögyam Trungpa.

(Continued on next page)

The Shambhala Dictionary of Buddhism and Zen.

The Spiritual Teaching of Ramana Maharshi, by Ramana Maharshi. Foreword by C. G. Jung.

Tao Teh Ching, by Lao Tzu. Translated by John C. H. Wu.

The Tibetan Book of the Dead: The Great Liberation through Hearing in the Bardo. Translated with commentary by Francesca Fremantle & Chögyam Trungpa.

Vitality, Energy, Spirit: A Taoist Sourcebook. Translated & edited by Thomas Cleary.

Wen-tzu: Understanding the Mysteries, by Lao-tzu. Translated by Thomas Cleary.

Zen Essence: The Science of Freedom. Translated & edited by Thomas Cleary.

The Zen Teachings of Master Lin-chi. Translated by Burton Watson.